THE LINE

THE LINE

A NEW WAY OF LIVING
WITH THE WISDOM OF
YOUR AKASHIC RECORDS

BY ASHLEY WOOD
WITH BEN WOOD

sounds true
BOULDER, COLORADO

Sounds True
Boulder, CO 80306

Published 2022

Cover design by Tanya Montpetit
Book design by Meredith March

The wood used to produce this book is from
Forest Stewardship Council (FSC) certified forests,
recycled materials, or controlled wood.

Printed in the United States of America

BK06210

Library of Congress Cataloging-in-Publication Data

Names: Wood, Ashley (Co-founder of A line within), author. | Wood, Ben
    (Co-founder of A line within), author.
Title: The line : a new way of living with the wisdom of your Akashic
    records / by Ashley Wood with Ben Wood.
Description: Boulder, Co : Sounds True, 2022.
Identifiers: LCCN 2021045647 (print) | LCCN 2021045648 (ebook) | ISBN
    9781683647836 (trade paperback) | ISBN 9781683647843 (ebook)
Subjects: LCSH: Akashic records.
Classification: LCC BF1045.A44 W66 2022 (print) | LCC BF1045.A44 (ebook)
    | DDC 133.9--dc23/eng/20211104
LC record available at https://lccn.loc.gov/2021045647
LC ebook record available at https://lccn.loc.gov/2021045648

10 9 8 7 6 5 4 3 2 1

This book is dedicated to my daughter Baboo,
the seed planted in me that sprouted my awakening.

CONTENTS

CONTENTS

THIS BOOK IS ABOUT A NEW WAY OF LIVING, A NEW
ORDER OF LIVING, A NEW WAY TO EXIST WITHIN
THIS DIMENSION WHILE ALSO EXPERIENCING OTHER
DIMENSIONS. THIS BOOK IS ABOUT EXPLORING WHAT
IT MEANS TO LIVE IN A MULTIDIMENSIONAL UNIVERSE.

- THE PINNACLE

FOREWORD

I don't recall exactly how Ashley and I met, who reached out, or when the first time was that we chatted. The only real recollection I have of our first connection is that our spark of sisterhood ignited though Instagram.

I somehow stumbled upon her work and resonated deeply with the message that she was putting out into the world. I believe that instant spark of sisterhood was a soul recognition. And though we have yet to meet in person, Ashley and I have shared many deep conversations through text, back and forth, over voice memos. I've always felt that I can share openly and honestly with her. I'm heard. I'm held. I'm grateful to call her friend.

I don't believe this is the first time Ashley and I have known one another. I'm sure our souls have known each other many times over.

I've actually never shared this with her until this very moment, but something tells me that we've come from the same place. Our souls implanted from somewhere out there in the great beyond, put here on this Earth to share the message of love during these challenging times. Before listening to Ashley's teachings and becoming aware of my "Line," I would have thought the deep knowing, the story of our two souls coming here to Earth at this time for a very specific mission, to be something of make-believe, but it's not. I'm certain of it.

The way Ashley teaches about energy and frequency has inspired me deeply. So much so that I have even included a line about the Pleiades in one of my songs, "Spaceship." Ashley has a beautiful gift and an even more beautiful heart. She is a powerful teacher. And most of all, she lives what she teaches. She is as authentic as they come. I'm so happy that she is sharing her gift in these pages. Get ready to know yourself, your soul, in a whole new way.

– LEANN RIMES CIBRIAN

INTRODUCTION

There is an energy point in the palm of your hands that is linked to your heart. This point is known as the heart of the hands, or the Talahridaya *marma* point in the ancient science of Ayurveda. If you hold out your hand and focus on sending love to someone, your palm can react to the energy you're giving and feel hot and tingly.

Right now, I am sending love to you. My palms are open and pulsating like a heart full of love and gratitude to you for receiving the energy I have infused in these words.

In this book, I'm going to teach you about another energy point in the body. It's called the Line, and it runs from the crown of your head, down the midline of your body, to the bottom of your feet. When you align with the energy of the Line, you will feel divine love running through you. This is the love we need to heal our wounds and see ourselves for what we are: stardust from the Universe, seeds of the Earth, souls spanning dimensions of existence, and beings with an intrinsic spiritual connection.

Through your Line, you're receiving specific instructions on how to show yourself this love. These are called messages, and they're running through your Line every second of every day. They're sent from a nonphysical realm called the Akashic Records. The Records contain the energetic imprints of everything your soul has ever experienced in this life and in every other one it's ever had.

Your Line is your direct connection to this realm. When you receive the guidance coming through your Line, you are accessing your soul's history to learn how you can live in alignment with the most authentic, compassionate, and embodied expression of your energy. This is called your Highest Self. When you use your Line, it is like you are communicating with your Highest Self on how you can reflect this divine expression in your life.

Your Line will help you navigate the small, everyday moments in alignment with your Highest Self and lead you to the gifts, purposes, and lessons your soul has brought into this life. This is the medicine your soul needs for its healing, growth, and evolution. Use it to heal yourself and heal the world. Your messages are infused with the energy of divine love, and when you act on them, you will feel supported by this love: lifted, guided, and empowered by your Highest Self. This love is like a lighthouse, showing you the path back to who you are meant to be in this life.

The Akashic Records are not a new concept. They have been around since energetic souls began to take physical form and have been accessed over time in a variety of different ways by people all over the world. I am going to teach you a new way of accessing the Akashic Records that aligns with the energy of our time. This is a new way of receiving and understanding how your soul is guiding you in this life.

We are living in a time that supports you on this journey. As a collective, so many of us recognize that the old ways of living and being are no longer in alignment with our highest good. For so long, we've been told who we should be, what we should think, and how we should feel to the point that we don't know ourselves anymore. More than ever before, it is important to come home to yourself; to the person your soul chose to be in this life. You are an individual beautiful expression of divine love, and you can use your Line to know this version of you.

The Pinnacle, the group of energies that I channel, have said, "When it feels as though you're in the dark, that's when you need to come back to this space of love and become even more aware of the whispers. Those messages that are soft subtle whispers, this is your guiding light home, back to yourself. Do you feel ungrounded? Unstable? Unsteady? That's because you're not home. Create a home within yourself. This is where you need to be. Ground into your home within yourself. This is where you need to be."

My promise to you is that by reading this book, you will learn how you can love and trust yourself enough to come home to your true self. This is a journey, but it's only the beginning; it doesn't end when you close this book. When you live a life in the Line, you show up every day with an awareness of how everything you say, do, and think can honor your connection to your Highest Self and the love flowing through you. You also feel your feelings, explore your triggers, heal your wounds, and commit with intention, reverence, and integrity to your soul growth, learning, and evolution.

On this journey, you will dive into your inner world and see how everything you feel is an invitation from your soul to get to know yourself. Every moment is a chance to look to the messages you're receiving through your Line for more information, for meaning or context, or for what to do next. You'll peel back your emotional layers, you'll experience your soul's connections to other places, times, and people, and you'll learn why you're here on Earth at this time and how your soul wants to grow and evolve in this experience. On this journey, you'll get to know yourself on a much deeper level than ever before and learn how you can move through challenging experiences and live a beautifully aligned, soul-fulfilling, and unconditionally loving life.

I'm here to guide you through a new way of living with the wisdom of your Akashic Records. I'll be holding your hand, but at some point while reading this book, I want you to put your hand over your heart so you can feel the love running through you. When you can show yourself this love, you can learn how to trust every message you receive and believe within your full essence that in this moment, you have everything you need to lead yourself.

HOW I LEARNED TO LOVE MYSELF

I've always known I was different, but I didn't always accept the things that made me different. For as long as I can remember, I've felt more energetic than physical. Since childhood, the dreams I've had of visiting different worlds and planets, meeting with deceased loved ones, and traveling through time and different dimensions of existence felt as real to me as my waking life. The way I felt the energy and love of animals was different from everyone around me. This is why when I was eight years old, I became the only (and possibly first) vegetarian in my small, conservative, farming hometown. I felt the wind differently; I felt the pulse of the Earth differently. I could sense and physically feel the emotions of others, even if they didn't express them.

I wasn't always able to explain these sensations and experiences, but when I did try to share this part of me with others, I would be covered in goosebumps, my heart would race, and my eyes would fill with tears. I felt as though I was opening a door within me, just a crack, letting the smallest glimpse of a big, bright light to shine through. The response was usually the same: "That's weird." For years I hid all of this deep inside while doing everything I could to appear "normal" on the outside.

I grew up in a small town in the province of Manitoba, in central Canada. The majority of the population were Christian and went to church faithfully, my family included. From an early age my grandma and I shared a strong bond. She was a devout Christian woman who was heavily involved in the church and never missed a Sunday service. She also had incredibly strong energetic gifts. She shared her crystals with me and would read my tea leaves, giving me accurate advice every single time. We would talk about angels and dreams, and she would tell me how her mother's spirit would visit her in the night. She was my first spiritual teacher and the first person who embraced and celebrated everything I thought made me different and "weird."

I was twenty-four when she passed away. I remember feeling quite sad, but by this point I also understood death as a transformation of energy, a rebirth, and I trusted she would continue to be with me always. My grandma showed me a new way of understanding spirituality. It was entirely different from what I had learned in church, and it helped me see myself with love rather than guilt, shame, or fear. Although she didn't publicly share her talents, especially with the church community, she told me, "Ashley, this is how God works through me. This is how I share God's love with others." This teaching has always stuck with me, and I hold it close to my heart. My grandma helped me see my abilities as divine gifts. After she transitioned from this physical plane, my grandma continued guiding me, even helping me discover how the Akashic Records are an important part of my purpose in this life.

I truly learned how to show myself love when I began paying attention to the messages I was receiving. This was before I knew what messages are or what the Line is. They would come to me as ideas in my head to take action—do this, read that, text this person—or confirmations that I was on my aligned path, like seeing repeating numbers (1:11, 4:44, 222, etc.) or hearing a ringing in my ear. I didn't realize at the time that these were messages coming from my Highest Self through my Line.

One night while washing dishes, I received two life-changing messages. The first was to start a podcast. The second was to begin sharing my spiritual gifts and experiences with the world. I had never done this before and didn't know how or why I would do it, what it would look like, or what would come from it. Our messages push us out of our comfort zone, but it is from our discomfort that we grow and transform.

Within a few weeks, I started the podcast and began talking about my spiritual experiences. A few months into the show I interviewed a guest who said I should learn about something called the Akashic Records. When she said those words, "Akashic Records," I felt strong energy run through my body, as if something that had been sitting dormant awoke. "What are the Akashic Records?" I asked her. "I've never heard of them." She said, "They'll change your life." I immediately bought a book about the Akashic Records that same day, and after reading only a few chapters I heard another message within me: "Put the book down, stop reading it. You have everything within you to begin this journey."

The Akashic Records are like a metaphysical library of everything your soul experiences from the moment it is created. Every action and every thought and emotion, conscious and subconscious, that it experiences in every life it ever lives is recorded in your Akashic Records. Accessing your Akashic Records provides you with infinite wisdom on your entire soul journey.

I entered my Akashic Records for the first time by closing my eyes, doing a brief meditation to center my energy, and reciting a prayer used to open the Records that I learned in the book. As soon as I entered, I knew there was no going back. The energy I felt within them had changed me forever and from that moment I was on a new path: my aligned path.

I quickly realized that I was connecting to a different energy than what I expected. I read in the book that I would be met by a unique group of energies whose role it was to guide and support me, but the energy I was working with felt different. It felt celestial. I was experiencing different realms, galaxies, and energies across dimensions. I couldn't quite describe it, but I knew my experiences were not "normal."

I practiced opening the Records for a few days but then stopped. I needed space to process and integrate the new energy I was working with; it felt beautiful but also overwhelming. One day, out of nowhere, I received a message to go into the Records immediately. Upon entering, I saw my grandma. She was standing with a group of celestial energies I didn't recognize. They told me that it is my soul's purpose to modernize the Akashic Records by making them accessible, approachable, less esoteric, and easier to understand.

From this point, I began dedicating my entire life to the Akashic Records. I went into the Records every day to learn more about them and myself, and within two weeks I began giving Akashic Records readings to clients all over the world. I released weekly podcast episodes sharing my experiences, and I was educating people about the Records on my social media. I later learned that the energies I channel in the Akashic Records are called "the Pinnacle," and they told me that they come from a star cluster called the Pleiades. The Pinnacle are also part of the Council of Light, which is a band of the highest dimension of cosmic energies that span across many points within the Universe.

It was through the Pinnacle that I learned about the Line and how to use it to access the Akashic Records without a prayer or grounding meditation. It's quick and matches the fast-moving energy of this time. Your Line gives you the soul context you need to understand and move through any situation you're in at the exact moment you need it. In the next few chapters, I will walk through the process of using your Line to access the information in your Akashic Records. When you become familiar with this process and the energy you're aligning to, receiving your messages of love, support, and guidance can become as easy as breathing. This information is flowing through you, and it is my hope that you use it to find your way back to yourself so you can lead yourself through life with aligned sovereignty, soul awareness, and empowerment.

From the moment I understood how the Line works, my life changed more than it ever had. I learned how to trust myself, love myself, and live a life aligned with my soul. I learned more about my gifts and my purpose. I learned what my soul brought into this life for my evolution. I learned how to manage my emotions, how to have perspective on any situation and experience, and how to live in the frequency of the Line, which is the frequency of love.

Through my Line, I am my own teacher, my own healer, my own guru, and my own guide. I live a life of peace, trust, alignment, and love for myself and others. This same transformation has happened for so many people in our A Line Within community who have begun working with their Line. Throughout this book, I will share examples and stories from members in our community, or clients whose Akashic Records I've read, that tell of the insight, love, and transformation the Line has brought them. These are people who have completed our online workshops at alnwithin.com, listeners of our podcast *The Line*, and our social media followers (@alnwithin).

Throughout this book, you will find exercises designed to help you use your Line to understand your energy and emotions, learn how to identify your messages, and practice integrating what you receive into your daily life. Receiving your messages is something you were born to do, but acting on your messages in the divine timing that you receive them is a learned skill. Most of the exercises include journaling prompts so you can describe what your energy, messages, and alignment feel like to you. Using your Line is a personal practice, and for this reason it's important to reflect on your unique experiences with your Line and your messages, so you can take your learning deeper and further your growth.

In this moment, you have everything you need to lead yourself. You have your Line, and you're receiving messages through it right now guiding you back to yourself, but it's up to you to do the work. Your messages share what you need to do in each moment to be in alignment. You don't receive the big reveals or the full transformation all at once. Your soul journey is a life-long, winding path, and your messages are the stepping stones. They will give you everything you need to know to take the next step so you can keep walking and growing. You may feel like you want more, but you must trust that in each moment you have everything you need to keep moving.

It's time for you to get to know yourself like you never have before. Your soul guided you to this moment and to this book. You're ready to start trusting yourself, guiding yourself, loving yourself, and living in alignment with who you truly are. I'm still holding your hand. Feel the warmth in your palm; our energies are connected. I've got you, but more importantly, you've got yourself.

CHAPTER 1

WHAT IS
THE LINE?

WHEN YOU HOLD A MIRROR UP TO THE SUN, IT
CREATES A GLARE, A VERY BRIGHT LIGHT. THIS IS HOW
POWERFUL YOU ARE WHEN YOU ARE IN CONNECTION
WITH YOURSELF. YOU ARE ON THIS JOURNEY FOR
A PURPOSE. ISN'T IT SO BEAUTIFUL WHEN YOU
DISCOVER THAT? NOW IS THE TIME TO SEE YOURSELF.

– THE PINNACLE

You were made from the stars and planted in the Earth to grow. Throughout your life, you remain connected above and below by an energetic frequency that runs through you called the Line. In every moment of every day, you are receiving messages of guidance, love, and support through your Line. These messages come from an energetic realm in the Universe called the Akashic Records and are activated by the life-giving energy of Mother Earth. When you listen to your messages, you will learn how everything you experience in this physical realm has its roots in the energetic part of you, deep within your soul. You are made of energy, and your soul will help you understand how this energy can guide you back to yourself so you can live along your aligned path.

The Pinnacle have taught me that energy is everywhere. It runs through all things and is always moving. They have said that energy has a heartbeat and that this is what we're measuring when we calculate joules or the Schumann resonances of Earth's electromagnetic field. Energy is all around us and, whether we're aware of it or not, we're interacting with it throughout our entire lives. Some people can see energy, others can hear energy, but we can all feel energy.

Your soul is energy, and it speaks to you through movements of energy that I call energetic vibrations. You may feel these energetic vibrations in your physical body as aches, tingles, or even changes in body temperature, but more predominantly, you'll feel it as emotions. The reason the soul has a physical life is to experience emotions and to learn, grow, and evolve from them in preparation for its next experience. Once the body has completed its natural biological cycle, the soul will take a new shape, either as another human life or as another expression somewhere within the infinite dimensions of our Universe. Energy is always moving, and the end of a physical life isn't the end of a soul.

What's exciting to me is that your soul isn't bound within your body or this physical realm. Your body is just one "space" in which your soul is currently existing in this present moment (and in all moments). The soul is multidimensional and is having infinite experiences, including nonhuman ones, on many different planes of existence, *simultaneously*. So at any moment, you can be receiving information from any of these experiences. Although these experiences are commonly referred to as your past lives, because this conforms to our human notion of linear time, they are all happening in the same *energetic* time.

Here's an example the Pinnacle gave. Imagine you're holding a porcelain plate. This plate symbolizes your energy. Now imagine that you drop the plate, and it shatters into many tiny pieces. One of these pieces is your energy in your physical body, in this physical life. The rest of the pieces are the other experiences your energy is having in different dimensions. All the pieces are on the floor at the same time because your energy is having this experience in your physical body at the same time as all the other experiences in this and other realms. Your soul exists concurrently on many different timelines. For this reason, I will refer to your soul's multidimensional experiences as your soul's other lives. See chapter 10 for a more detailed explanation.

Information from these soul experiences is stored in your Akashic Records, and if there's something from any of them that can help you (there always is), you will receive this information as a message through your Line. You've been receiving these messages every day, all day, since the moment you took your first breath, and they'll continue coming as long as your heart is beating and your lungs are breathing. I call them messages, but you may know them as your inner voice, intuition, gut feelings, or sixth sense. These messages support your soul's growth and evolution and help you learn how to move through your life in harmony with the highest and most aligned expression of yourself.

You can think of your Line as a filing system that contains everything you need to guide you in this stage of your soul's journey, including discovering your purposes and gifts and learning about the specific things your soul chose to work through and learn from as part of its continual evolution. When you live life in your Line, you will be empowered by your messages to be your best teacher, your most motivational leader, and your own healer. It's all within you. This is a new way of living.

HOW THE LINE WORKS

In this life, you are both energetic and physical, and your messages reflect this duality. They begin as energetic transmissions from the realm where your Akashic Records are stored. Your messages enter your body through the crown of your head. At this point they are pure energy because they come from a purely energetic realm. After running through the midline of your body (your Line), they exit your body at the base of your pelvis, which is also the base of your Line. From this point, the energy enters the Earth, and the life-giving energy of Mother Earth activates and brings your messages into the physical realm so you can receive them.

Once activated, your messages contain the wisdom of your soul's history (your energetic essence) and the grounded knowledge to guide you in this life on Earth (your physical essence). After passing through the Earth, your messages come back up and enter your body again through your feet. They then run up your legs and through your Line where they become available to you. This is an automatic and continual process that occurs so quickly that at any given point in your day, even right now as you read this book, you're receiving messages.

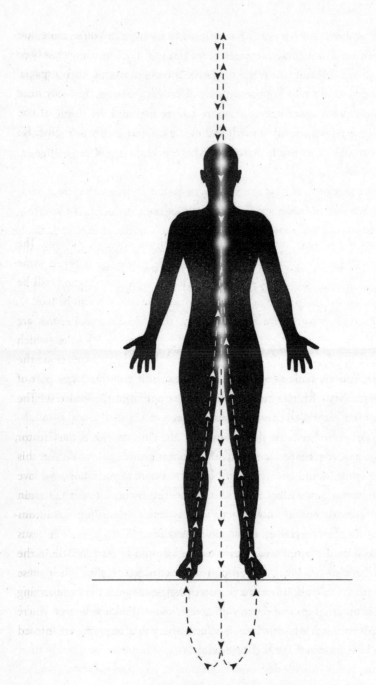

THE PATH OF THE LINE

If all of this is new to you, I want you to know that you're more connected to your Line and your messages than you think. This energy has been with you since the moment you were born. You don't need to learn a special skill to receive your messages because it's already happening. You only need to shift your awareness back to yourself and also toward the magic of life! You have everything you need within you to begin living with your Line. It's time to come home to yourself and your energy.

WHERE ARE YOUR MESSAGES COMING FROM?

As I mentioned earlier, your messages come from your Akashic Records. The Records are governed by the Pinnacle, who act as gatekeepers. When someone enters the Records, the Pinnacle will decide what information will be shared and what that person's experience within the Records will be like.

The Pinnacle have communicated to me that the Akashic Records are stored in a star cluster in our physical Universe called the Pleiades (which will be discussed more in the next chapter) and that they themselves are the highest form of Pleiadian energy. The Pleiades and the Pinnacle are part of the highest realm, which contains many other points in the Universe. The Pinnacle have also called this realm the Council of Light.

Imagine this realm as the step below God, the Universal One, the Creator, the Divine, or whichever name you're most comfortable using. Within this realm are energies and cosmic beings of the highest vibrations of pure love from infinite points within the Universe and multiverse. From the main stars and galaxies that we know in our solar system (Sirius, Orion, Andromeda, etc.) to the energies of well-known Ascended Masters such as Jesus and Ganesh (two examples who have worked alongside the Pinnacle in the Records through my Line), are all part the Council of Light. When these energies come through, it is not a person or religious figure I am connecting with. It is an energetic expression of divine love—the same energy you're connected with through your Line. The messages you're receiving are infused with the love energy of the highest realm.

WHO IS SENDING YOUR MESSAGES?

In every message, you are receiving exactly what you need to know in that moment to act as the most aligned, loving, and divine version of you. This version of you is called your Highest Self. In a sense, you're being guided by the highest expression of you.

Your Highest Self is your most important guide. It is the purest form of your energy. Although it does understand human emotion, it doesn't hold on to pain, trauma, or wounds from any of your human experiences. Your Highest Self is the energy of pure love. This is why your soul looks to your Highest Self for guidance. Although your soul is also an energy, it feels human emotions because it wants to learn how to process them. Your soul carries joy and pain, healing and wounds, and triumphs and trauma from this and its other lives. When you follow the guidance of your Highest Self, you can understand how to respond to your emotions and experiences for your soul's higher learning and evolution. This is why I call this work "soul growth."

In addition to your Highest Self, your cosmic support team also includes all the energetic guides that support you throughout this stage of your soul's journey, including other energies from the Council of Light, celestial beings and star energies, ancestors, deceased family or friends, spirit animals and, of course, the Highest Power—God, Creator, Divine, Universe, whatever language you prefer to use. Some guides will be present throughout your entire life, while other guides are with you only for certain chapters of your life.

Think of your Line as a braid of energetic strands. There's one strand for your Highest Self, another for your cosmic support team, and a final one for your human mind. Your Highest Self sends the messages, your human mind interprets them, and your cosmic support team is available to you through your Line for any additional guidance or support you need to help you act on your messages and live in this physical realm. Every strand of this braid plays an important role.

I have had many experiences in the Akashic Records in which the most important guide that showed up in a client's reading was their Highest Self. I could tell that their cosmic support team was present, but they were observing from the sidelines, and it was the Highest Self taking the lead. This was an important breakthrough for me and my clients to make—you really do lead yourself. And it is the same with your Line. Your cosmic support team is supporting you and your Highest Self. Take full credit and remember to thank yourself for the messages coming through your Line, the action you take on them, and the realizations and growth that come from this. It's all you.

ARE YOUR LINE AND YOUR AKASHIC RECORDS THE SAME THING?

Your Line connects you to the realm where your Akashic Records are energetically stored, and you're receiving guidance from this realm every moment of every day, but this does not mean you're "reading" or "in" your Akashic Records every moment of every day. I have taught thousands of people around the world how to read the Akashic Records, and even though the messages are coming from the same place, the process of working with the Records is quite different from using the Line. To formally enter the Records, I practice and teach my students a more ritualistic process. It begins with reciting the Prayer of the New World and involves adhering to a set of guidelines and maintaining devotion and commitment to developing your ability to receive information over time.

I channeled the Prayer of the New World on April 30, 2020, when as a collective we were moving through an era-defining moment of change. Delivered in aligned timing by the Pinnacle, this is a prayer of compassion that supports deep introspection and self-healing. It's a prayer of cosmic and Earth energy that takes us to an entirely new realm within the Akashic Records. This prayer channeled through me but does not belong to me; it belongs to us all. While I use it to access my Akashic Records, I also teach it to our students who are learning how to read the Records, and it's available for you to use as well. You'll find it at the back of the book in the appendix. If you're inspired, give it a try!

The Pinnacle taught me about the Line so I could teach you a quick and easy way of accessing the information within your Akashic Records without a formal practice, prayer, or ritual. Energy is moving fast, messages are coming through quickly, and the Line matches the speed of our time by providing guidance in the exact moment you need it. It can also give you a moment of pause so you can find presence and stillness within yourself and receive clarity in any situation.

There is a difference between using your Line to receive information from the realm of your Akashic Records and formally entering your Akashic Records. Think of it this way: your Akashic Records is a house and your Line is the yard. Both aspects of the property are important, and both serve their own purpose. They complement one another. By standing in the yard, you can receive a lot of information about the space. You can feel the grass beneath your feet. You can see flowers, vegetable gardens, trees, and shrubs. You can walk on the sidewalk or the driveway. You can see the house's shape, color, and street number. When you look in the windows, you can see all the contents inside, all of the artifacts that hold the energy of life, from framed photos to pieces of furniture. You get a sense of its overall architectural design. You can see if there are any people inside or if pets live there.

Now imagine using a key to unlock the door and enter the house. Just like that, you've gained a new depth to this experience. Your senses are activated with heightened awareness; you can inhale the smell of each room, touch the fabrics, and open the cupboards and drawers. The information you get inside the house supplements and enriches everything you learned standing in the yard.

One of the major differences between the Line and the Akashic Records is that the information you receive through the Line is just for you. It's a frequency that is connected to your Akashic Records only, nobody else's. You may receive guidance on a situation that involves other people or the relationships in your life, but the guidance is always for your soul evolution and growth. When you actually enter the Akashic Records, however, you can access other people's Records (with their consent), as well as your own. You can also read the Records for animals, buildings, or land.

The two practices go hand in hand, and those within our community have found great support in using their Line as their main source of information and then supplementing with the Records when needed. The Line is so accessible, actionable, and convenient! Your Line is always on; there's nothing to enter, no prayer to recite. This information is always flowing through you. You can receive and act immediately.

LIVING IN ALIGNMENT

The Pinnacle encourage us all "to be an active particle of light in the full anatomy of this collective experience." To fully shine as all that we are, we must live in alignment with the person our messages are guiding us to be. Imagine that every person on the planet is a pixel of color. Everyone has a unique hue or shade that represents the essence of their soul: the expression of their unique purpose, gifts, wounds, growth, and love. It is a composition that everyone brings with them into this life.

When you hold the intention of living in alignment with your Highest Self and are aware of the beauty of this physical experience, the divine love flowing through everything, and the fact that you're here on purpose for a purpose, your pixel of color is illuminated. When every person lives with the intention of being in alignment, the individual pixels light up to form a beautiful mural. To be of service to the collective, to be part of "we," you must be able to connect to "me," for the collective cannot shine as brightly if you're not lit up. You matter, and you are here at this time for a reason.

Alignment isn't a permanent state of being, and it doesn't look the same for everyone. Alignment is a feeling available to you in each moment, and whether or not you experience this feeling is based on the things you do, say, and think. Your messages will tell you what you need to do to be in alignment, but these things will change from moment to moment. Living in alignment is learning to be aware of and responsive to how your messages are guiding you.

You have an energetic frequency and so does your Line. While your Line's frequency never varies, your frequency changes based on your overall emotional state. We experience energy in our bodies as emotion and when you shift your frequency to match the frequency of your Line, you will feel this as a change in your emotional state.

This doesn't mean you escape your emotions. You are designed to feel the full spectrum of emotions, from joy to anger, from peace to grief. Your Line doesn't prevent you from feeling; it opens you up to understanding what your feelings are here to teach you. When you know the reasons for your emotions, you can learn how to move through them without being controlled by them.

The frequency of your Line is your energetic constant, your lighthouse, your North Star. It's always available to you because it's always running through you. Your Line gives you a new perspective, a sense of calm, gratitude for the hardships, love for yourself, and, of course, messages from your Highest Self. Follow them when you need to find your way.

Your messages give you actionable advice on how to balance living your day-to-day life as a physical being (learning how to understand, manage, process, and release your emotions) with what you need as an energetic being (how to use your gifts, live out your purpose, and learn how your soul wants to grow in this experience). This is what it means to live a life in the Line, and this will look different for everybody, but the first step in this journey is the same for everyone: learning how to shift your energy to match the frequency of your Line so you can receive your messages. You can do this with an exercise called Line Activation, which I will discuss in detail in the next chapter.

Your messages are delivered to you like droplets of water—slowly, subtly, softly, and consistently dripping into your awareness, one by one. The Pinnacle have said that if you act on your messages, you'll find yourself swimming in an ocean of ease. If you ignore them, you'll always be thirsty.

An ocean of ease isn't a false promise of an easy life. It means that you'll learn to see your moments of challenge and struggle as opportunities for growth and evolution. You will still feel all the beautiful and difficult emotions, and you won't know what's to come, but you will have a larger understanding, awareness, and gratitude for the experience you're moving through.

When you release expectations of what your life should look like or the kind of person you should be and surrender to the guidance you're receiving from your Highest Self, you can trust that you'll move through every experience in the most soul-aligned way. It's not always the easiest way, but it's the path of your transformation.

The soul does not grow and you do not deepen your relationship with yourself from "easy." The soul grows from awareness, experience, and the contrast of energetic highs and lows. Your messages provide you with the insight you need to understand what you can learn in every situation and how you can move through every experience like you're swimming in an ocean of ease. "You can know a lot," the Pinnacle have said, "but you cannot know everything." Within this beautiful, miraculous gift of life, there will always remain some mystery.

If you ignore your messages, you'll always be "thirsty" for guidance, direction, understanding, meaning, connections, and love. Feeling thirsty is what it feels like to be out of alignment. You may feel restless, like you're never content in the present moment. You may look to others to decide what you should do or who you should be. You may judge others or chase a life you see others living instead of the aligned one that will fulfill you on a soul level. This is an uncomfortable feeling.

Your messages show you that you have everything you need to live in alignment within you, but you're not expected to do everything for yourself, by yourself. We all need love and support, and when you're aware of what your body, energy, mind, and soul need at any given moment, you will sometimes be guided to people who can support you further. I work with a few different intuitive healers whom I value and trust. I know exactly when I need a session with one of them; I can feel it in my body, and I also receive it as a message through my Line.

You can also be guided to people in your life whose support aligns with what you need in that moment. These can be spouses or partners, family members, or friends. When you show up in these relationships in alignment, you can seek the support you need without unfairly offloading your energy onto them. Your messages will help you manage your energy in a healthy way so you can receive advice and support from a place of awareness and alignment.

Every moment of love, guidance, and support you receive through your Line moves you along an aligned path. Every step you take helps you shine a little brighter as your unique and divine energetic expression. You were born on purpose and with a purpose, and part of your soul's journey in this life is to discover and live out this purpose. Your messages can lead you to your purposes, and they can also reveal the unique gifts your soul brought with it into this life and the lessons it has come into this life to learn. Your purposes, your gifts, and your lessons are things you live out and work through every moment of every day.

There is no order in which you'll discover these things about yourself, but the more you use your Line, the more you will discover about them. Your Line provides you with limitless information, guidance, and practical advice that is unique to you, your soul journey, and your life purpose. You only need to start receiving the messages that are coming through your Line 24/7.

Once you align with the frequency of your Line, the energy within you is transformed. Your energetic communication with the Universe shifts. And with this shift, you're presented with an opportunity to change your entire life.

Are you ready to learn more? It's time to activate your Line and your awareness of these messages flowing through you. I'm still holding your hand. Feel my energy as you read these words. I'm here to guide you and support you until you're ready to begin trusting that everything you need to know is available to you through your Line.

CHAPTER 2

HOW TO
ACTIVATE
YOUR LINE

TAKE TIME TO KNOW YOURSELF. TAKE TIME
TO BE YOURSELF. TAKE TIME TO LEAD
YOURSELF. TAKE TIME TO LOVE YOURSELF.

- THE PINNACLE

The Line Activation is a simple practice that combines deep breathing and a few short repetitions of arm movements. The purpose of the Line Activation is to activate your awareness to the energetic frequency of your Line and the messages flowing through you, enabling you to receive them with clarity, efficiency, and speed. The breathing centers your energy, and the arm movements mimic the flow of the Line through your body. It's like turning your awareness on.

Activating your Line is the light-speed version of accessing your Akashic Records because it gives you direct, immediate access to the same frequency as the Records. You can receive information on everything from how to get through a stressful day to the beautiful gifts and purposes your soul brought into this life.

The Line Activation is the key practice throughout this book. It is integrated into the exercises and the teachings, and I encourage you to integrate it into your daily routine so you can gain the full benefit of this book. Living in the Line is a lifestyle that requires consistent awareness and attention, and just like any new practice, you will receive back what you bring to it.

While you're learning this practice, I encourage you to activate your Line at least once a day, in addition to the Line Activations you complete for the exercises in this book. I find that beginning your day with a Line Activation can help set your intention or realign your energy before moving ahead. But you can also do it before you meditate, as an afternoon break, or at the end of the day.

Listen to the guidance you're receiving and be spontaneous enough to activate your Line at the precise moment you feel called to do it. Don't second guess yourself; just do it. The more you practice, the stronger your awareness becomes and the more open you will be to receiving your messages. This practice is about you and your energy. Make it your own by doing what feels right for you in the moment.

EXERCISE LINE ACTIVATION

Begin by getting comfortable in a standing or seated position and bring yourself to the present moment. Close your eyes and take a few deep breaths in and out of your nose. If it supports you in centering yourself and quieting your mind, you can imagine a bright white line of light running from your head down to your toes, illuminating your body with divine energy. I like to do this, but Ben doesn't, so play around with what works best for you.

1. Breathe and move to activate.

With your eyes closed, place your palms together in a prayer-like position a few inches in front of your body and raise them above your head. Inhale deeply through your nose for a count of four to six seconds, then exhale through your mouth for another count of four to six seconds, keeping your hands above your head the entire time.

Inhale again through your nose and this time, as you exhale, slowly move your hands down the midline of your body, keeping them a few inches in front of your body the entire time.

Your hands will naturally begin to part around your midsection. Keeping your middle fingers touching, inhale and press your hands back together while moving them back up your body and returning to where you began, with your hands over your head. When you've done a full up-and-down movement, you have completed the first sequence.

If it's more comfortable for you, you can inhale as you move your hands down and exhale as you move them back up. Since each inhale and exhale should last for four to six seconds, move your hands slowly enough to reach their final destination (above your head or at your midsection) by the end of the breath.

Repeat four up-and-down sequences to activate your Line. An instructional video is available for you to watch at alnwithin.com.

2. Sit in activation.

After completing the movements, keep your eyes closed, place your hands by your side or in a prayer position at your chest— whatever is comfortable for you—and continue breathing at your normal rate through your nose. This is called sitting in activation. You are present, you are in meditative stillness, and you allow yourself to be and receive.

When you sit in activation, you may notice a shift in your emotions, awareness, or overall energy. You may feel the frequency of your Line, whether as a sense of calm, larger perspective on a situation, or deep love for yourself or others. During this time, you may also ask your Highest Self for guidance or clarity, but we'll talk more about that in the next chapter.

LINE ACTIVATION FAQS

WHEN SHOULD I ACTIVATE MY LINE?

You can activate your Line anytime, anywhere. This is a practice that you can fit into your life, not something you need to fit your life around. I encourage you to make this practice part of your daily routine. Outside of your regular Line Activations, you may also want to activate your Line if you're feeling disconnected from yourself, if you want to feel calm and centered, if you want to feel love, if you need perspective on a situation you're going through, or whenever you feel called to do one.

Our community has brought this practice into their lives in so many interesting ways. One person said, "My very first Line Activation changed my life. It was empowering to feel my energy, fully trust the messages I was getting, and to follow my intuition. Daily Line Activations have been the biggest reason my spiritual journey has evolved to where it is now. It instantly grounds me. Anyone can do it, just about anywhere, and that is the beauty of it. It has been such a gift, contributing to my overall wellness, and I am so thankful for this practice."

Many yoga teachers in our community lead their students through a Line Activation to center their energy and return to the present before beginning their class. Nurses in our community have shared that in 2020, when they began their shifts with a Line Activation, they would often receive messages to take care of themselves during those physically and emotionally difficult times. Some artists in our community like to complete a Line Activation before painting, writing, or creating. And parents (like me) do Line Activations with their children to either diffuse a moment of tension or teach energy management and self-connection.

One parent in our community said, "Doing daily Line Activations has created the peaceful space that our home desperately needed. I've shared your teachings with my husband and daughter and have taught them how to create a sense of calmness with the Line Activation. My four-year-old may not know exactly what she's doing, but when she sits with me, we are in complete harmony for the few minutes we do our Line Activations. Shortly after, there's a sense of balance and tranquility. Not a day goes by without doing our Line Activations, and I personally have had more downloads than ever being in line with my true self."

HOW LONG SHOULD I SIT IN ACTIVATION?

When you're first starting this practice, I encourage you to sit in activation for at least five minutes so you can get to know how this energy feels to you. Make a mental note of how you felt before your Line Activation and compare that with how you feel while sitting in activation. It's important to give yourself enough time to feel the frequency of your Line in your physical body, whether you feel this as a change in your emotional state, clarity on a situation, or reception of a message.

Overall, the intention you have for activating your Line will determine how long you sit in activation. If you're activating your Line to align your energy, sit until you feel that shift in your energy and emotions, like you're stepping out of your present moment to gain perspective and feel calm. If you want to receive your messages, sit in activation until you receive them. We'll talk more about your messages, what they are, and what it feels like to receive them in the next chapter.

DO I NEED TO BE SITTING DOWN TO SIT IN ACTIVATION?

You can sit, stand, or lie down. Find a comfortable position that supports your awareness of your messages and the frequency of your Line.

HOW WILL I FEEL DURING AND/OR AFTER MY LINE ACTIVATION?

The Line Activation will offer you peace, calm, and perspective, and sometimes it may provide you with an emotional release. You may feel this as tingling within your body, as if your senses are awakening and activating. You may feel a lightness in your head, an expansion of your heart space, or an extension of your spine. Your hands and feet may tingle or even slightly burn. These are all indications of energy activating within you and are safe physical responses.

Depending on how open or closed you currently are to your energetic body, you may feel pressure in your head and neck while doing your Line Activation or sitting in activation. Some community members feel unsettled and a little afraid when this happens, and they close themselves off to this energy. I want to reassure you that if this is your experience, it's part of the natural process of opening up and releasing stuck energy. The more you continue this practice, the lighter you will feel from it.

Imagine opening the door to a room that's been shut for years. The air in the room feels thick and heavy, and you need to force the window open.

But within a few minutes of airing out the room, the atmosphere becomes light and clear. The Line Activation creates a lot of flow and movement of energy throughout your body, and you must allow this process to happen. You're working with your energy throughout this practice; this is you and only you. Surrender to yourself.

CAN I ACTIVATE MY LINE IF I'M FEELING LOW?

I once heard from a community member who thought they shouldn't do a Line Activation if they felt emotionally low. This isn't the case at all. Your emotions are your energy talking to you. Acknowledge what you're feeling, don't fear it, and use a Line Activation to find the deeper reason for your emotions.

Even if you feel so low that you can't hold the sincere intention to feel activated by this practice, I still recommend doing a Line Activation because the movement and breathing alone will move energy around in your body. This will shift your frequency, which you'll feel as a change in your emotions, even if only momentarily, and will therefore activate your awareness of a different frequency within you. This practice doesn't require you to show up feeling your best, but it can help you shift your energy so you can feel your best.

CAN I DO MORE OR LESS THAN THE FOUR SEQUENCES OF THE ARM MOVEMENTS?

The Pinnacle shared with me that great transformation is completed in series of four and that this mirrors the four-season cycle in many parts of the natural world. You should be completing the four sequences, but you can do more if you need more time to align with the frequency of your Line. I recommend remaining open and aware of your needs each time you do a Line Activation. You may complete the four sequences one time, but the next time you may need to do eight or ten before noticing the shift in your energy. Everybody in our community practices their Line Activation slightly differently. Within their practices, there are regular variations as they respond to the energy they're feeling at the time.

DO I HAVE TO DO THE ARM MOVEMENTS AT ALL?

You may find yourself in a public setting where you need to manage your energy but don't feel fully comfortable doing the arm movements, and in these cases focus on your breath and set the intention to return to the frequency of your Line. If it helps, close your eyes and visualize energy running up and down your Line. Your intention is always what matters most.

WHAT IF I CAN'T VISUALIZE?

Over the years, I've had members in our community share that they cannot visualize. If this is the case for you, I want to assure you right now that you can still do this work. This is all about awakening your physical body and syncing it with the energetic frequency of your Line. If the word *visualize* is confusing or discouraging for you, I invite you to replace it with *daydream* or *imagine* (like you're thinking of your favorite place on Earth or recalling a cherished memory).

It's also important to mention that holding a vision takes focus, practice, and determination. If you're new to visualization, your brilliant and busy mind may likely do anything it can to distract you. Your ego, fears, or other thoughts may cloud or alter your vision. Work on this as you would to develop any other skill. I will discuss this throughout the book.

WHEN WILL I START RECEIVING MY MESSAGES?

At first, you may just feel a sense of calm and comfort without any messages coming through, and that's okay. That's more than okay. Celebrate whatever your experience is and trust that as you continue to practice Line Activation, your connection to the frequency will grow and change.

It's important to practice the Line Activation without an expectation of when messages will come through for you or what they'll be about. Instead, pay attention to the energy you're aligning with as you activate your Line. What does it feel like to you? How did you feel before activating your Line? How do you feel after? The Pinnacle have said to "use your emotions as your compass." Notice how you feel before, during, and after each Line Activation.

I will talk more about messages in the next chapter, so for now, as you practice your Line Activations, remain open, receptive, and present to anything that's coming through for you during and after your Line Activation. This practice supports you in opening your awareness to the frequency that is always flowing through you all day, every day, not only when you're activating your Line.

I've noticed that the longer I sit in activation after doing a Line Activation, the more clearly I receive messages throughout the day. Sometimes I won't receive my messages until after I've spent time in activation, or perhaps they'll appear an hour later or even in my dreams that night. The practice is intended to activate your awareness of your Line, to flip the switch to on so you're actively in receptive mode.

WHAT IF I DON'T RECEIVE MESSAGES RIGHT AWAY?

Whenever people ask me this question, I say to them, "If you decided to learn a new language today, would you expect yourself to be fluent tomorrow?" You're learning a new language within yourself, your soul language, and if you've never paid attention to it, it can take time to fully receive and believe it. Give yourself patience and space to grow within this practice. It will come, I promise, because it is you. This is all within you.

WHAT IF THOUGHTS CROSS MY MIND WHILE I'M DOING MY LINE ACTIVATION?

Welcome them, observe them, and embrace them. The Line Activation practice isn't about having a still, silent, and quiet mind. It's about receiving everything that's coming through for you, including your thoughts, because your messages are often within your thoughts. Your mind plays a key role in translating your messages, and so your thoughts, both conscious and subconscious, are important to observe during this practice. Everything you receive during your Line Activation, even your thoughts, has a deeper meaning. Allow it all to come through.

YOUR ACTIVATION POINTS

On your body, there are two energetic Activation Points where your Line and your messages enter and exit your body: the Universal Activation Point at the crown of your head where the energy of the Universe enters your body, and the Earth Activation Point at the base of your feet where you connect to the energy of the Earth.

The arm movement sequence of the Line Activation mimics the flow of the messages coming down from the realm of the Akashic Records and entering you through the crown of your head, running down your body, and exiting at the base of your pelvis before moving into the Earth and then back up your body through the soles of your feet.

While the Line Activation practice shifts your energy to match the frequency of your Line, you can also cultivate a connection to these two Activation Points to strengthen your awareness of this frequency. Universal and Earth Activations describe the energy and emotions you receive from these two points that bring you back to the divine love flowing through you.

UNIVERSAL ACTIVATION POINT

The Universal Activation Point is your connection point to the realm of the Akashic Records, where this energy and your messages are coming from. The realm of the Akashic Records is an energetic one, meaning you can't see it using your physical eyes, but you can see the points of the physical Universe that surround it.

The Pinnacle have said our Akashic Records are stored in a star cluster called the Pleiades. They've also said that this is their energetic home, which is why I channel them in the Records. They like to communicate through the number 4, and it's therefore no coincidence that the Pleiades are located 444.2 light-years from Earth. You can locate this star cluster in the night sky from every point on Earth. Look for the constellation Orion and then draw a line from Orion's belt past a large red star called Aldebaran until you see a small cluster of stars. This is the Pleiades. Even though it's a small cluster, and even on the clearest night they're not the brightest stars in the sky, the Pleiades have been an important universal fixture that humans have long been attracted to.

The Pleiades are not visible year-round, and their appearance in the sky (roughly from November to April) have been observed as a significant dates in the calendars of many different civilizations throughout human history, marking seasonal or temporal shifts, bringing reminders of when to begin certain agricultural tasks like planting or harvesting, or signaling important religious days.

For some peoples in the Society Islands in the South Pacific, the calendar is split into two distinct seasons corresponding to the Pleiades' rising on the Eastern horizon and setting on the Western horizon. The Iroquois divide the year into male and female halves, with the Pleiades' appearance in the sky marking the beginning of the female half of the year.[1] The ancient Greek poet Hesiod wrote in his poem *Works and Days*, often described as an early farmer's almanac, that when the Pleiades appear in the night sky it is a reminder to work the land, and when they set in late October or early November, it is a reminder to "plough in season: and so, the completed year will fitly pass beneath the earth."[2] Many other peoples, including the Guaraní of Paraguay and the Blackfoot of North America, use the Pleiades to determine agricultural practices.[3]

The Pleiades are also prominent in the stories, mythologies, and folklore of different cultural groups on almost every continent throughout history, including many different indigenous peoples of the Americas, Aboriginal Australian peoples, and ancient European civilizations going back as far as the Bronze Age. In 1999, an ancient artifact dated to 1600 BCE called the Nebra Sky Disk was discovered. On this bronze disk are embossed symbols representing a waxing crescent moon, the sun, and the Pleiades star cluster, making this the oldest known map of the stars to have been discovered.[4]

The Pleiades have been an important source of wisdom, guidance, and understanding throughout human history, and I believe this is because within these stars lives the home of the Akashic Records. Everything our souls have ever experienced is stored here, and we're drawn to this energy. When we look up at the Pleiades, we see a part of ourselves.

The next time you look up at the night sky, see yourself within the stars, as if you're saying to the Universe and yourself, "I know my soul draws me here, my Line connects me here, and I'm receiving pure divine love and guidance from this realm." Feel the energy coming to you and receive it in your body as love, joy, amazement, and connection. This is what it's like to receive a Universal Activation.

The energy and emotion you receive is turning your awareness on to your intimate and innate connection to the stars. If you have never located the Pleiades in the sky before, pay attention to how you feel the first time you do. If you have seen them, pay attention to your emotions the next time you see them. These emotions, even if they're subtle, are important. You are from the Universe, and you hold a piece of the Universe within you. These Universal Activations remind you of that.

Have you ever felt little butterflies in your belly or your heart flicker while watching a sunrise, the brilliant hues of red, pink, orange, and yellow cast across the dark land, bringing forth the light of a new day? Have you felt a whoosh of energy within you when you see a shooting star or find a planet in the night sky? Have you ever felt the magic of watching the magnificent northern lights dance across the sky? What about seeing bands of light break through clouds as the sun sets on the horizon? These sunbeams, sometimes referred to as crepuscular rays, are also called "God's rays" and the sight of them feels miraculous. These are all moments of Universal Activation, and opportunities to feel the beauty of the Universe in your physical body.

There are also times when significant alignments of the stars and planets will cause shifts in your energy and emotions and your ability to connect with your messages. Although we can feel the effects that all the planets have on our energy, you can experiment with our moon. Next time there's a full moon, a new moon, or a full or partial eclipse, pay attention to your emotions and your energy. These events are heightened times to receive Universal Activations through your Line.

EARTH ACTIVATION POINT

We hold a sacred, soul connection to the natural world and our Mother Earth. Although you are an energetic being with an intrinsic spiritual connection to the Universe, your soul chose to have this human experience here on Earth, and the energy of the Earth supports you by playing a special role in allowing you to receive your messages.

When your messages come down from the Universe, they are pure energy. They must enter the Earth for you to receive them. During this process, the Earth translates these energetic transmissions into intelligible messages that you can receive in the physical realm. Since the Earth's energy activates every message that comes from the Akashic Records, your soul's history (and the history of all souls) is not only stored in the realm of the Records, but also in the Earth beneath our feet. Connecting to the Earth grounds you in your physical body, on this physical plane, while also connecting you with your energetic self.

You can receive Earth Activations by making an intentional connection to the Earth and remembering that your energy is stored within it.

Activating this connection grounds you, heals you, and brings you back to yourself and your messages.

Have you ever had your breath taken away simply by being in nature? Have you ever felt the tranquility of looking out upon endless flat prairie land or felt the Earth's power by standing at the base of a colossal, majestic mountain range? Have you ever stopped to listen to the sound of ocean waves crashing against rocks or taken in the silence of the ethereal stillness of a pond? Have you reveled in the feeling of fresh morning dew on the bottom of your feet or the sound of a large body of water singing as it freezes or of the wind whistling as it blows through swaying trees?

The best way to connect to the Earth's energy is to go outside, no matter what season it is, and breathe deeply. Feel the temperature of the air as it enters your lungs and moves through your body. Embrace the warmth of the sun shining on your face. Receive the drops of rain or flakes of snow as they touch your skin. Take off your shoes and let your feet sink into the ground. Run your hands through grass, sand, or dirt and make a physical connection to the Earth. This will help clear your mind and ease any tension that's stored within your body.

Whether you're in a forest far away from people or living in a large city, commune with nature. This may look like a walk through a park or simply touching a tree planted next to the sidewalk. Talk to the trees, animals, flowers, wind, and sky, either with your voice or energy. Everything holds consciousness, and you'll receive communication from the natural world when you open yourself up to it. If you cannot go into nature, close your eyes and imagine your feet rooting into the ground. Feel thick, strong tree roots growing from the soles of your feet down into the ground below.

You can connect to the Earth during any season. I live in one of the coldest places in Canada, and we can experience winter-like temperatures for up to six months of the year. The land and water freeze and are covered in snow, and the temperature can plummet to -40°F and sometimes even colder. When you surrender to the discomfort of the elements, whatever that discomfort looks like to you, and allow the guidance from your Highest Self to flow through you, you can discover unimaginable beauty, release, and freedom. You are reminded that you can overcome anything you're presented with. If the Earth can freeze and then months later be reborn, if a forest can be decimated by fire and soon after sprout new life, then so can we move through the seasons of our lives.

You can also bring plants into your home and spend time caring for them. Water them, prune them, touch the soil, and even talk to them. This will support your Earth Activation year-round.

Another way you receive Earth Activations is from the food you eat. By eating "close to the Earth," as the Pinnacle have put it, you nourish your physical and energetic bodies. Eating close to the Earth means consuming foods that have come from the Earth, like fruits, vegetables, nuts, and seeds. Consuming these foods in their true, unprocessed form (or as unprocessed as possible for you) grounds your body in the Earth's energy because they were given life in the Earth. Eating in season, however that looks where you live, also supports your connection to the Earth.

By noticing the intricate and divinely designed details of Mother Nature in whatever way you can, you are receiving Earth Activations. It's that simple. You remember who you are at your physical root and energetic core. Once you start to explore the infinite and expansive love that Mother Nature provides, your awareness of the energy of your Line heightens, and it becomes easier to shift into this frequency so you can receive all the messages flowing through you.

CHAPTER 3

HOW TO RECEIVE YOUR MESSAGES AND TRUST WHAT'S COMING THROUGH

YOU WALK WITH GREATNESS; YOU WALK WITH
KNOWING; YOU WALK WITH EVERYTHING NOW THAT
IS SHOWING. DON'T HOLD YOURSELF BACK, DON'T
HIDE YOURSELF AWAY. TAKE THAT KEY AND OPEN
YOURSELF UP, NOW IS THE TIME, TODAY IS THE DAY.

- THE PINNACLE

When I was in my late twenties, I worked at a bank. I was on the wellness committee and was always looking for ways to integrate small changes to improve the workday for my colleagues. I remember one team meeting in particular when I led everyone through a recording of a guided meditation.

I closed my eyes and drifted off into another dimension, feeling at the end that I had received the perfect midday realignment. When I asked others how their experience was, the majority of my colleagues said they spent most of the time with one eye open, looking around to make sure they were "doing it right" and not being open to experience for themselves the relaxation or the brief pause that a guided meditation can bring. The concept was simple: sit in your chair with your feet on the floor, close your eyes and breathe deeply. However, for many in that room, this was very difficult.

It wasn't the instructions that people found challenging. It was trusting that whatever the meditation looked like and felt like to them was "right." How many times have you been in a situation where rather than believing in yourself, you looked to others for confirmation that what you are doing, thinking, or saying is correct? When we look to others, we distract ourselves from the truths we each hold. By doubting our abilities and awareness, we make very simple things difficult. One of the main purposes of this book is to teach you how to trust yourself. The first step toward this is to stop looking outside of yourself. When it comes to trusting yourself and receiving your messages, there is no standard of "normal" against which you need to compare yourself. Your experience is going to be beautifully unique to you and in order to learn everything I share with you in this book, you must begin by connecting to yourself, to your emotions, your thoughts, and your experiences and trusting that all of it can help you align with the person your soul chose to be in this life.

The most commonly asked question I receive from people is how long they need to do Line Activations before they begin to receive messages. The short answer is that there are *always* messages flowing through your Line. If you feel like you're not receiving them, it may be because you aren't paying attention to your energy and don't notice when you are receiving or even acting on your messages. You don't have to learn how to receive messages. You need to learn how to recognize the messages that are already coming through.

WHAT IS A MESSAGE?

A message is guidance from your Highest Self, an energetic transmission just for you and delivered in divine love the exact moment you need it.

This guidance or support will look different from person to person as everybody is on a journey that is unique to their soul. Even your messages will change depending on where you are on your journey or what kind of day you're having. The one thing that doesn't change is the energy of a message. This energy is divine love, the vibration of your Highest Self, and the same energy running through your Line. This is also the same energy of the realm of the Akashic Records. You're in constant connection with this energy, and with every decision you make, you're either responding to this energy (your messages) or you're not. Your messages don't come with a loud alert announcing their arrival—*incoming message!*—which is why it's so important to learn what the energy of a message feels like to you.

Generally, there are two different aspects of a message—the communication you receive and the energetic feeling you experience. The specific communication you receive is the "content" of your message, its meaning to you and your life, and it can be about anything. You can receive guidance on how to make a change in your life, prioritize yourself, move through a difficult situation, or diffuse a tense situation; information on someone to connect with or reconnect with; the reason for a difficult experience in your life; confirmation that you are where you need to be; or anything else that shines light on who you are at a soul level and helps you act as your aligned self. Your messages are clear, often quite simple and actionable. Even a message like "Be still" requires you to do something—namely, to slow down, notice, observe, be aware and, as delivered, to practice stillness.

Your messages are designed to bring you closer to yourself so you can walk in trust, peace, confidence, and reverence with your soul's aligned path. They can be subtle and gentle whispers, giving you general reassurance or support. They can also be very specific like "Text this person," "Send this DM," "Go into this store," or "Share this piece of information." They can relate to anything in your life, like an idea for a new creative project, a reminder to do something you've been putting off, or clarity on why you feel tired, physically unwell, or anxious. I could make a list the entire length of this book and still not include all the possible messages you could be receiving or what they're telling you right now—only you know this. For that reason, I encourage you to complete the exercises in this book so you can experience for yourself what kind of messages you're receiving.

There will be times when you won't immediately know how a message relates to you, your soul, or your life. It may take a few hours, days, weeks, or even months to make the connections and put all the pieces together, like a big jigsaw puzzle. This is because you receive your messages in steps or as small puzzle pieces. Your messages are drawing from everything your soul has experienced and is experiencing on other planes of existence, and it can take time for your physical body to process this information and apply it to your life. The Pinnacle have taught me that we always receive exactly what we need to know the moment we need to know it and not an ounce of information more or less. It's common for members of our community to have an "aha!" moment about a message (what it means and why they received it) only after moving through the specific experience that the guidance they received was for or by making a connection between their message and something in their past—in other words, by putting the puzzle pieces together.

Your messages are full of wisdom, but you still need to do the work of understanding how they relate to your life in the moment you receive them. This requires introspection, awareness, and a knowing that everything is connected to everything else. Your past is connected to your present, your present is connected to your future, your future is connected to your past. This is a really beautiful moment of self-realization, or as I like to call it, soul realization, because it helps you see divine purpose, where before you might have seen coincidence.

WHAT DOES A MESSAGE FEEL LIKE?

I like to describe the feeling of receiving a message as an inner knowing. It's a moment of reconnection to your soul-self, illuminating what has always been there, a reminder of something you already knew but didn't realize until that moment. Sometimes messages feel like something being brought back into your awareness in a way you can't immediately put into words. Other times, they come as a total surprise. All the same, a message is a feeling of confirmation of who you are on a soul level, the connection you hold with yourself and clarity on the next step to take.

You can also feel the energy of your messages in your body in many ways, such as feeling light, rejuvenated, or excited. You can feel your messages in your heart, filling you up with love, in your belly, like a gut instinct, or as other noticeable shifts in your mood or emotions. And even though they're delivered in love, they can sometimes feel painful, like a headache or jaw tension, indicating energy and emotional healing that needs to be released to create space within your energetic body.

The feeling of a message also includes how your messages come to you. There are many ways you can receive a message. You may hear it, see it, feel the emotion of it, or have a memory from this or another life. They can be bold, like specific guidance in the form of a thought in your mind, or subtle, like seeing a number that confirms something you've been thinking. Have you ever noticed 1:11 on the clock or paid for something that cost $4.44? Maybe you constantly wake up at 3:33 a.m. or find yourself always driving behind license plates that contain double or triple numbers such as 111 or 555. These number patterns are commonly called "angel numbers," and it's believed that each number pattern means something specific. However, it is not only the number itself that's bringing you a message but the thought you had in the moment you saw it and what happens after. The next time you see a number pattern, pay attention to your emotions and your thoughts. What were you thinking about and how did you feel in the moment you saw the numbers? Then pay attention to how you feel after seeing the number. Your Highest Self is showing you these numbers to support your brain in translating a message that is coming through for you in that moment. The numbers are helping you "see" the message, highlighting its importance so you can make connections to how it applies to your life.

You may receive the same type of "signals" or "signs" from your Highest Self through song lyrics and even the words that other people say to you. These signs can also highlight, confirm, or draw attention to the messages you're receiving through your Line. The ways in which you can receive them are limitless, so it's important to have your awareness turned on. Remember: everything is energetically connected. Nothing is an accident; nothing is a coincidence. You're in constant communication with your Highest Self and your cosmic team.

When people are just beginning to use their Line, they will often say that they don't receive messages because they're not intuitive, psychic, or spiritually gifted. The truth is that you don't need to consider yourself an intuitive or a psychic or be an experienced practitioner of any spiritual modality to receive your messages. You only need to know your energy and be open to the many different ways your messages come to you. You were born to do this. Your Line, your mind, and your Highest Self (plus your cosmic team) are braided through you for a reason. Be open to anything that's coming through and trust that you will learn to know when you receive a message.

The way you receive a message will depend on your energy at that moment, and since your energy is always moving, the way you receive a message will, too. Don't get distracted or overwhelmed by how you receive messages; allow yourself to naturally understand your process by regularly sitting in activation and becoming familiar with this energy. When you activate your Line, focus on the energy running through you and open your awareness to everything your senses experience. Don't write off anything that comes through, however small or insignificant it may seem. One message is not greater than another. No matter how big or small it may seem, each message you receive holds the same energetic weight, and you are receiving it at the perfect time.

Another reason why people don't believe they can receive their messages is because they are listening to their ego, not their messages. The Pinnacle have said that the ego is primal human energy and that it does everything it can to protect you, which can sometimes mean preventing you from new and unfamiliar experiences—in other words, growth. This can mean that your ego will want you to continue familiar patterns even if they're pulling you out of alignment with your Highest Self. It will do this by telling you that you're making up your messages, that you can't or aren't ready to do something different, or that you're not worthy of the guidance you're receiving. None of this is true. Your messages are sent just for you and delivered in divine timing, at the precise moment you need to receive them and are ready to follow through on them.

People will also disregard their messages as mere coincidences in a random and chaotic Universe. However, when you trust that you're always receiving messages at the exact moment you need them and that you're an active part of the Universe—that you not only come from the stars, you're made of stardust—you'll see that nothing is a coincidence. Every message is divine guidance, every moment of chance or coincidence is intentional, and every connection you make brings you closer to your soul. Nothing is an accident; everything has meaning, everything is connected.

IS IT A MESSAGE OR YOUR MIND?

When you begin paying attention to your messages, you may, like many in our community, wonder what the difference is between the activity in your mind and the messages coming through your Line. I commonly receive questions like, "How do I know if it's a message or if it's my mind making something up?" I understand the confusion and can empathize with where this is coming from because it's so easy to doubt ourselves and question our intuition. So let me offer three simple words to help you: trust your mind. Trust your mind if it's encouraging you. Trust your mind if it's exciting to you. Trust your mind because it's translating for you.

Your messages are your intuition, an inner knowing. But first and foremost, they're energetic transmissions, and your brain helps you translate this energy in order for you to understand it. Messages do not come with language. Your brain applies your language to them so you can receive them as a communication. This translation process happens so incredibly fast that you don't notice it, but at all times your brain is working hard with your Highest Self and your cosmic team to deliver this guidance of support and divine love to you. The subconscious mind and conscious mind are always receiving and as long as you feel encouraged and supported, entertain it, allow it. Your brain is brilliant and a key player within all of this. Don't write off your thoughts or realizations if they're not sparkly and goose-bump (or "truth-bump") worthy. Not all messages will "feel" energetically exciting. In fact most of them will be incredibly subtle.

Just as your mind is deeply connected to your soul, it's also working with your ego, which is your primal human energy. Your ego wants to keep you "safe" in familiar patterns, thoughts, reactions, and beliefs. In keeping you safe it wants everything you do, say, and think to remain the same. When you receive a message, your mind makes two translations. The first translation is your message. It will be delivered in energetically neutral but supportive language, without the energy of fear, judgment, or pressure. It will provide grounded, loving guidance and will feel "right" to you. That said, your messages may push you out of your comfort zone by offering you a new perspective, reaction, or insight. Your mind will translate your ego energy second and this energy will try to prevent you from taking action on the

41

message you received. It will do its best to hold you back from believing it and keep you within your comfort zone. It's important to be able to distinguish the difference between the two energies because your mind is working with both your soul and your ego. You want to be aware of both energies so you can learn how your ego keeps you out of alignment and what you can do to feel safe and supported when you're responding to your messages. I will discuss the ego more in the next chapter.

EXERCISE RECEIVING YOUR MESSAGES

It may seem counterintuitive, but the best strategy for receiving your messages is not to think about them. When you look to your energy for the *actual* messages instead of to an idea of what messages you *think* you should be receiving, it's easier to spot what's already coming through. You are energy, and energy is always moving and changing, so be open to receiving whatever messages come through and in whatever way they come through. The following exercise will help you focus on your energy so you can trust the messages you're receiving right now.

1. Say the mantra.

Stand in front of a mirror, look at yourself directly in the eyes, and say out loud, "I receive my messages." Looking into your own eyes is like looking into your soul. It's incredibly powerful, and it can also be very emotional. Speak these words with the belief that you're receiving messages right now. Speak them with love. Speak them until you start to feel an emotional encouragement deep within your heart.

2. Activate your Line.

Do a Line Activation as described in chapter 2, and as you complete the breath and arm movement repetitions, repeat the above mantra in your head.

3. Sit in activation.

As you sit in activation, feel the energy of the Line in your body connecting you to the realm of the Akashic Records, where your messages come from. When you feel ready, ask the following question: What is one way I can show up as my Highest Self today?

4. Journal.

Your message may have come through as something you heard, felt, visualized, or simply knew deep within you. You may have received a long answer or one word, or maybe you felt an energetic shift. This experience can sometimes be so subtle, like a soft whisper or split-second inner knowing, and your ego can quickly write it off as something you made up or a random thought. Your messages can sound like your own mind or inner dialogue. Trust that you received everything you needed at that moment, even if what you received didn't make sense at the time. Use the following prompts to help you understand and trust what you received:

What message did you receive?

How did this message come through? Describe your experience.

Optional: If you don't feel like you received anything, or doubt what you received because it felt too small or insignificant, or if you don't feel like you noticed any shift in your energy, the following prompts will help you become more aware of your energy and your messages.

As you reflect, be gentle, show yourself love, and write without judgment.

While sitting in activation, did you feel any change in your emotions or energy?

Did you allow yourself to surrender to this energy or were you scared or hesitant to fully let go and trust?

What thoughts did you have while sitting in activation?

YOUR EMOTIONS ARE YOUR
ENERGETIC EXPRESSION

Messages are energy, and when you receive a message, you can feel the energy it carries. It's the same energy you're aligning with in a Line Activation: the energy of the realm of your Akashic Records, your soul, and your Highest Self. I encourage you to commit to developing your Line Activation practice, so you can spend consistent time in this frequency and learn what it feels like to you. When you're able to notice the difference between how that energy feels compared to how your own energy feels at any given moment, it will become easier to identify your messages.

We experience energy in our physical bodies as emotions, and each emotion you experience has an energetic frequency. When you feel fear in your physical body, for example, the frequency of your energetic body changes to match the energetic expression of this emotion. Your emotions reveal how you truly feel about a decision you're making, a situation you're in, or a dilemma you're having with family or friends.

But they are telling you even more than that. Your emotions are your clue to the energy you're holding, and this energy may be the reason you're struggling to trust the messages coming through (fear, for instance, makes it harder to trust your divine guidance) or the reason you feel out of alignment with yourself. This is because the energy of your emotions can pull you out of alignment with the energy of your Line. Your soul incarnated into this life to evolve by experiencing and learning from the range of human emotions. You will and should feel your emotions, but you do not need to be controlled by them. As the Pinnacle have said, "Observe your emotions but do not become attached to them. They are not yours; you do not wear them." Your Line can help you observe the emotions you're feeling in your physical body and then release them so you can align your frequency with the energy of your Line and receive guidance from your Highest Self on how to move through any situation with perspective and clarity.

Acknowledging your emotions is the first step to releasing them and adjusting your frequency. This may mean breaking subconscious patterns or ingrained habits that you unknowingly use to prevent you from getting to know yourself. One thing to be very aware of is that our devices (phones, iPads, tablets, etc.) can keep us from knowing our emotions and energy. Despite all the advantages technology brings us, we often use it to distract us from ourselves and our present situation. When you're stressed, overwhelmed, or upset about something, do you take time to process what you're feeling, or do you open social media to disconnect from whatever is happening in your life and connect with someone else's?

In your day-to-day life, are you paying attention to the emotions you're holding? To how you feel about the things you say, the people you spend time with, and the activities you devote your time to? Do you notice when your mood shifts? Do you know what sparks the change? It's easy to know your emotions when you experience intense anger or happiness, but what about all those subtle emotional shifts you experience throughout your day? Every single thought you have has an emotion attached to it. Consider how many thoughts you have in a day, and you can easily see how many different emotions you're regularly experiencing.

After acknowledging your emotions, the next step is to look for the source of this energy. Sometimes the source of our emotions can seem hidden from us, but that's often because instead of looking deeper within ourselves, we choose (consciously or subconsciously) to feed the energy that's making us feel this way. When you're angry, do you try to understand why, or do you look for things that reinforce this feeling? You may do this without realizing it, like scrolling through angry content online, diving deep into a comment section of insults, or sitting in your emotions without processing and working through them. It can sometimes seem easier (and even justifiable) to look for ways to feed your uncomfortable emotions rather than confront the reason for them.

You can also feel energy as physical sensations in your body. Your energetic and physical bodies work together. Sometimes you need your physical body to "speak up" in the form of a physical sensation to clue you in to your energy and even to messages coming through. Common sensations are jaw soreness, headaches, or minor muscular discomfort. But pain is not the only telltale sensation. You can also feel love as a warmth in your chest, or experience a release of tension and a state of calm as if heavy energy has literally melted off your body, after you complete a Line Activation or make an important connection between your emotions and a message you received. Your emotions and physical sensations are a reaction to energy moving through you, and this energy is trying to tell you something. It too is a message. Nothing you feel is a coincidence.

You were born with an innate connection to your messages, and your Line Activations will help you remember this. As you develop your practice, you'll become more familiar with what this energy feels like to you. This will make it easier to distinguish your messages from everything else that's going on in your day. Eventually, you may even begin to notice that you receive messages as soon as you shift your awareness to this energy with the intention of receiving guidance from your Highest Self. The more you pay attention to your emotions and the feelings within your body, the more you'll be able to make connections between what you're experiencing and what it means for you and the situation you're in. Trust your feelings, trust your energy, and trust what you believe it means. Trust is the only way to truly know yourself.

Throughout this book, I will continue encouraging you to love yourself enough to know yourself, your emotions, your energy, and your soul. I'm still holding your hand, and in the chapters ahead, I will be walking you through a gentle process of how to know your energetic self. Before moving onto the next exercise, I want you to say to yourself out loud, "I love myself enough to know myself." Try to feel these words as you say them—or even better, look at yourself in a mirror, keeping eye contact with yourself as you speak. If you feel you need more support in knowing how you're feeling in this current moment, I recommend completing the following exercise.

EXERCISE GETTING TO KNOW THE ENERGETIC YOU

There are many people in our community who, most of the time, don't take the time to understand how they feel. If this is you, love yourself for arriving at this point—your messages led you here, whether you were aware of them or not—and for committing to knowing yourself better than you ever have. This exercise will support you in opening up your awareness of how you experience energy in your physical body. Consider it an energetic check-in to prepare you for the following chapters.

1. Connect to your heart.

Find a comfortable position, either sitting in a chair or lying on a bed, and release any tension you're holding. Place your hands on your heart, close your eyes, and take a few deep breaths. Notice the air as it moves through your body. Feel your heartbeat beneath your hands. Allow your body to sink into your seat or bed, and your forehead, jaw, and shoulders to soften. Stay in this position as long as you want. When you're ready, proceed with the rest of the exercise.

2. Journal.

Use the following journal prompts to explore the relationship between your energy, your body, and your current life situation:

Describe a recent experience that had a big impact on how you are feeling emotionally and energetically right now.

How did this experience make you feel? Describe anything you've been feeling, such as fatigue, vitality, aches, strength, anxieties, numbness, excitement, or fear.

3. Activate your Line.

End this exercise by doing a Line Activation with the intention of receiving your messages on the changes you can make in your current situation to improve how you feel in your body. If you're still feeling fear, what can you do to release that energy? If the experience you wrote about made you feel excited, what can you do to feel that way more often? Sit in activation for as long as you need to, trusting that every answer you need is available to you through your Line. When you're ready, ask your Highest Self, What is one thing I can do right now to shift my energy? Write your message in your journal and follow through on the guidance you received.

CHAPTER 4

HOW TO TAKE ACTION ON YOUR MESSAGES

THE MOST BEAUTIFUL, POWERFUL EXPERIENCES THAT
YOU WILL HAVE REQUIRE YOU TO DO SOMETHING.
YOU SEE, YOU MUST DO SOMETHING. YOU CHOSE
TO BE IN THIS PHYSICAL BODY TO DO SOMETHING.

- THE PINNACLE

The most important gift you can give yourself is the dedication to knowing yourself and how your soul wants to grow and evolve in this stage of its journey. Your messages support you in this self-soul discovery. You can use your Line to understand why your soul chose this life at this time and to discover the purposes and gifts you've come into this life with and the lessons your soul is ready to learn. While this doesn't mean your life will be free of challenging moments, it does give you the tools to move through every experience with understanding, love, and perspective, and this helps you grow as a person and supports your soul evolution.

Your messages are opportunities to learn more about what your soul wants in this life. It's the work your soul signed up for before this physical experience, but it's just that—*your* work. You are free to choose which messages you'll act on and when you'll act on them. You're free to decide if you're ready to act on a message, if you want to do a Line Activation to learn more, or if you won't follow through on it at all. And, of course, you decide every moment of every day how you're carrying your energy, how you're responding to your emotions, and how you're treating yourself and others. Within every moment is a choice, and you're receiving guidance on how to move forward in alignment with your Highest Self. I encourage you to acknowledge your messages as you notice them, even if you don't act on them, by saying to yourself, That was a message. This will help you trust that you are receiving messages and learn what they feel like to you and the many different ways they can come through.

Your messages are coming from a realm of unconditional, eternal divine love, and because of this, you won't stop receiving your messages even if you never act on a single one. You won't be energetically punished by God or the Universe if you ignore them, and no matter what, you won't have to ever prove your worth to receive them. Your messages will always be running through your Line and guiding you back to your soul-self. However, you will feel both physically and energetically out of alignment when you ignore them. It is a sacred practice to love yourself and trust yourself enough to be guided by your soul. Very often, it's easier to continue doing things the way you've always done them. But your messages are showing you another way, another more aligned version of you. "Come back home to yourself," the Pinnacle have said. "This is the only way. No one can tell you what to do; no one can tell you where to go; no one can tell you what it is within that you must show. This is within your dreams; this is within your heart; this is within your energy; it is now time to start."

You are receiving messages to support your growth and to grow you'll need to be pushed out of your comfort zone. You won't always feel like you have everything you need to take the leap or that you're ready to act when you receive the message. This is why it's important to love yourself for every small step you take, even if that means just processing the information you're receiving. It's the little things—the small, consistent changes you make in your life, the slight adjustments in your perspective—that lead to profound growth.

STEP INTO WHO YOU ARE

Several years ago, Ben discovered he had a cyst growing in his throat. I had learned from the Pinnacle that there's an energetic root to every illness and disease, and often it's connected to a life our soul is having elsewhere. The reason this experience manifests as a physical symptom, illness, or disease in this life is to learn about it, grow from it, heal it, and release it. I shared this with him, along with what the Pinnacle had said to many of my clients with similar physical symptoms in the throat: he needed to start using his voice and speaking his truth.

At the time, Ben was on a journey of rediscovering who he was and embracing his soul-self. He felt stuck in life and realized he had outgrown many things including his job, beliefs about the kind of person he could be, and ideas about what he could achieve in his life. Since energy is always moving, emotions need to be felt, expressed, and released (not ignored or repressed) in order to support the energetic flow within the body. Feeling "stuck" can result in an experience of continual emotional trauma, and unless this is addressed, healed, and released, the energy is suppressed in the body and eventually manifests into physical symptoms. A physical symptom is also considered a message; the body is always working with the Line to communicate with us what it needs. From everything I'd learned in the Akashic Records, from the Pinnacle, and through hundreds of client readings and experiences, I believed that if Ben spoke his truth and made the changes in his life to support it, the energy in his throat would move, and the cyst would disappear.

As I was building a business by giving Akashic Records readings to clients, Ben was starting to reflect on his own spiritual journey throughout his life. He grew up in a religious home and regularly went to church until his early twenties, when he was in college and started to see the rational, intellectual side of himself as incompatible with his spiritual beliefs. He felt like he couldn't be both smart and spiritual, so he made a choice and left the church. The information I was channeling in the Records offered him a new perspective to understand his spiritual path. He was receiving messages encouraging him to embrace his spirituality, but he also felt stuck in his old mindset. Slowly over the next year, he worked through this identity crisis by changing these ingrained and limiting beliefs about the kind of person he could be.

As my business grew and I learned more from the Pinnacle, he was able to help me understand everything I was receiving and communicate it with my growing community. This was what it looked like for him to use his voice, and he felt energetically different when he did. It also helped him learn more about his soul-self and discover his gift of translating and communicating complex information. About one year after discovering the cyst, Ben left his full-time job to start our company, A Line Within. He had been receiving messages for many months to leave his job and join me in business, but he was very reluctant for a number of reasons. He didn't know if we would make enough money to cover our bills. If he stayed at his job, where he was comfortable but wasn't fulfilling the potential his Highest Self had been showing him, we would at least be guaranteed a paycheck every two weeks. He also didn't know what it would look like to work from home with me and our daughter always there. On top of that, he had never started a business before—neither had I—and he wasn't sure he would know what to do. So, it was a considerable leap for him and a huge exercise of trust in the messages he was receiving to leave his job and start this business with me.

As the cofounder, he has many roles, but all of them at that point were behind the scenes; I was the face of the company. By helping create the content but not joining me in sharing it, he felt he was doing enough to use his voice and share his gifts. But he kept receiving messages encouraging him to be more public with the company. Sharing this side of himself with thousands of people pushed him far out of his comfort zone. It made him feel exposed, vulnerable, and uncomfortable. He feared what other people would say, especially people he personally knew.

Around this time, we purchased a home outside the city and spent most of the summer clearing the overgrown vines that covered the property. I learned in the Akashic Records that the house is on sacred land that supports creation, and that our cleaning of the land supported energetic clearing within ourselves. This is why Ben would often receive his messages when gardening or trimming overrun brush. The land, his Earth Activation, was speaking to him: "You know how to speak your truth. Use your voice with the company, go on the podcast, be more involved. Now is the time." By this point, Ben had started to read his own Akashic Records and he used them to learn the energetic roots of his fear and how the energy of his cyst was connected to one of his soul's other lives. He discovered that his fear of publicly stepping into himself was connected to a life his soul was experiencing in eighteenth-century Japan. In that life, showing who he was and using his voice put him in danger, so he hid in order to be safe. The energy of this experience had come into this life to be healed and released.

After making this connection, he began to appear on our podcast and social media occasionally, and we made many changes to our own workflow so he could be more publicly involved, including cowriting this book with me. At some point during this time, the cyst in his throat healed, solely by acting on his message of using his voice. He had addressed the energetic root before it could become a more serious physical health problem. On top of that, he experienced massive personal growth in his spiritual journey and was able to step into himself and his gifts in an entirely new way.

All of Ben's messages were delivered in divine timing, and although his soul was ready to act on them immediately, it took a bit longer for him to follow through. The reasons why Ben didn't act on his messages right away are the three most common reasons why people in our community don't act on their messages. These are: listening to your ego, not your messages; wanting to know everything that's going to happen before you take action; and looking outside of yourself to feed your doubt, insecurities, or fears. At some point, one of these reasons may be why you're not acting on a message. In the sections ahead, I'm going to teach you how to work through each of these so you can learn how to flow with the divine timing of your messages.

LISTEN TO YOUR MESSAGES, NOT YOUR EGO

According to the Pinnacle, "The ground is where the ego lives. This is where the messages come up, and that is where the first instinct is to keep yourself safe and deny yourself movement. Stay safe, stay safe, stay safe. The soul wants to grow; the human wants to stay safe. Once you break past that, once you break free, you move up toward the heart and then up toward free.

And when you're moving up toward free, that is the crown of the head where the messages keep going and flowing, and it's continuous instead."

Your soul wants to grow. It's designed to grow, and your messages support this by gently pushing you out of your comfort zone so you can be in new situations, have new experiences, and learn more about yourself with each step. You don't learn as much when everything stays the same. This means your ego aims to keep you from doing anything different, like breaking old habits or beliefs, experiencing unfamiliar situations, or confronting new emotions or perspectives.

When you allow your ego to take the lead, it will convince you that your messages are just your mind "talking" to you, that it's something you made up and should be ignored. The time between your message coming through and your ego responding is so slight they can feel indistinguishable at times. But you can tell them apart by remembering that your messages are support- ive, loving, and gentle. Your messages are honest but not harsh; they don't judge you or others, and they don't cause you to doubt yourself, your gifts, or your purpose. And even though your ego tries to keep you safe, this doesn't mean that your messages will put you in danger. They guide you to do things differently (but not recklessly) and will always provide you with loving sup- port that keeps you physically safe while nudging you toward soul growth. Sometimes acting on your messages requires you to do nothing. When we hear the word *action* we automatically think "doing," but action can mean doing nothing. Perhaps you're used to always "doing," and so your messages are now telling you to slow down, to be still, to observe, and to learn. Your ego wants you to keep "doing," but your soul wants to remain still. Taking action here requires stillness.

Acting on your messages means trusting that you are receiving divine guidance for your soul. An easy way to identify whether you're responding to your ego or to a message is to write down your messages. Sometimes going back over a message later in the day is all you need to see things differently so you can push aside your ego and trust yourself. You can also sit in activation, feeling the supportive and loving energy of your Line, to help you see the patterns you fall into, the familiar ways you do things, or the usual way you evaluate your plans or goals.

EXERCISE LISTENING TO YOUR LINE, NOT YOUR EGO

1. Play a game of trust.

It's time to play a short game so you can experience how your ego responds to your messages. I'm going to ask you a question. After reading the question, immediately note the first thing that comes through to you. That will be your answer.

Where are your soul's other lives on Earth taking place?

2. Journal.

Which locations came through before your ego doubted or questioned your message? This is your answer. There is no way for you to confirm this outside of yourself, of course. You must trust that the answer lies within you.

The deeper you dive into your process of receiving messages, the more comfortable and confident you'll become in overcoming your ego and trusting what you receive. Use the following prompts to reflect on how you experienced your messages, ego, and emotions while playing this game:

How did your message come through? Did you hear the name of a country or "see" a location?

What did you feel within your body when you received your message (e.g., chills, nerves, excitement, fear, etc.)?

How did your ego come in to doubt your message? What did it "say"? How did you respond to what it was telling you?

GET COMFORTABLE IN THE DARK

Your messages are invitations from your Highest Self to do something. The invitation tells you everything you need to know at that moment, but you don't know what will happen next. You don't know where your messages will lead; you don't know how you'll feel or what changes they will bring. Acting on your messages is learning how to be comfortable not knowing everything your ego is trying to tell you that you need to know before taking action.

Think of your messages like stepping stones in your soul's journey. You can see only far enough to take your next step, but each one takes you a little farther down a dark path. You are like a seed in the ground: your growth begins in the dark. As the Pinnacle have said, "There's nothing to fear about the dark. The dark is a place of knowing because when there is no distraction, the truth is there for you, revealed and showing. Find comfort in the dark." Walking this path requires you to trust that you will be given everything you need to know to continue walking and that you will receive only what you can handle. At every stage, you're supported by your Highest Self and guided by the wisdom of your Akashic Records for your growth and evolution. Surrender to each moment, trusting that you're receiving everything you need to know.

We often prevent our natural flow by worrying whether our interpretation of our messages is right or wrong, or we tell ourselves that we're waiting for more confirmation—from a guide, a friend, another message, an oracle card—before we act. Yet, you have everything you need at this moment to act on your messages. You can use external supports, like oracle cards for example, to help you understand your messages. We have many people in our community who do this, but the oracle card isn't giving you the confirmation; you are already receiving your energy, and the card responds to that. Pendulums act the same way: they read your energy and will confirm whatever energy you're holding with their swing. External tools can support you in developing your trust and confidence in yourself and what you're receiving, but the decision about what to believe or how to interpret your messages comes from you, always. Your journey is full of many paths, and there is no right or wrong path when you see every experience as an opportunity to learn more about yourself, your messages, and your soul.

There are also community members who say they are receiving many messages and don't know where to start or which one to respond to first. If you're following your messages, you can trust that whatever choice you make or message you act on first will be an aligned decision. But within that alignment, there are many possibilities—this is the beautiful gift of life! Ultimately, not even your Highest Self can decide for you. You need to decide, and you need to take responsibility for that decision.

FOCUS ON YOURSELF

When you're in the dark, it's tempting to look outside yourself for guidance or answers, to see what other people are doing or ask how they think you should respond to your messages. It's deceiving to think that by comparing your situation with someone else's, you'll receive more insight on what you should do. As tempting as it is to try to use other people's experiences to shine a light on your situation, this can very quickly pull you out of alignment and away from your messages. You grow in the dark because you're focused on yourself and your messages.

I'm often asked by our community how to stay focused on yourself when acting on your messages makes you very different from everyone around you, or when the people in your life question the guidance you're receiving. When you start following through on your messages, you may shed old patterns and habits that people assume are your true character traits. You may reveal parts of yourself you had always kept hidden from others, or you may make what seems to others like impulsive changes in your life. When you take action on your messages, you will change; that's the point of doing this work. These changes don't have to be drastic, and they may not happen all at the same time, but when you're committed to the guidance from your Highest Self, you won't stay the same. You're an energetic being that has come into this life to grow. Sometimes these changes may cause confusion or concern from your family and friends, resulting in uncomfortable conversations. Have compassion and love for yourself through the process and understanding of where others are coming from, while also zooming out on the situation to see the larger impact your messages have on your life. Remind yourself that change brings growth, evolution, healing, and greater understanding of your soul journey in this life.

Your messages will guide you to release things in your life that don't support your growth, and this often includes anything you do, say, or use that numbs you from this beautiful physical experience. I use to love drinking red wine, and it wasn't until I got pregnant that I realized how much of my social life revolved around alcohol. After having our daughter and continuing to avoid alcohol, I saw how this small change in my own life rippled throughout my entire social circle. As a new mother, I was receiving a lot of messages through my Line not to drink. But I would also receive comments like, "Now that the baby's out, you can have your wine!" I thought that I could carry on my life the way it was before becoming a mother, but I couldn't. I had changed, and many of my old habits were no longer in alignment for me.

Weeks passed, then months, then years, and I still wasn't drinking. One by one, my friendships that centered on alcohol naturally came to completion and were released. No longer were their conversations or company aligned with the spiritual growth I was experiencing and the direction my life was taking. I say this with complete gratitude for these meaningful relationships but also acceptance for their completion. I often felt lonely and sad about drifting from my friends, but I didn't regret my choice to stop drinking. I had to allow these changes to happen to continue down my spiritual path, where I would eventually discover the Akashic Records and step into my purpose in this life.

Releasing alcohol was an important message that I didn't fully understand at the time. I wasn't receiving it to understand why certain friendships felt like they no longer fit or to give me energy for the demands of early motherhood. When I first started reading the Records, one of the Pinnacle's rules for entering the Akashic Records was to do so with a clear and sober mind. This meant not having alcohol or mind-altering substances twenty-four hours before entering the Records. Because I was abstaining from alcohol already, when I discovered the Records in 2018 I was able to jump right into the practice, entering the Records daily (sometimes several times a day) to learn as much as I could. My mind was clear, and I was able to channel and receive messages with great clarity. You'll notice that when you're following your messages as they come, you may not know where they're leading you or what they're preparing you for. But when you look back, you can see that every message is divinely designed, and that every decision you've made, every message you've taken action on or ignored, has provided you with an opportunity for deep learning and growth.

EXERCISE A DAY OF ACTION

You were born with the ability to receive messages, but acting on them is a skill you need to develop. And as with all skills, you improve with practice. For this exercise, you will practice taking action on your messages for an entire day.

1. Choose a day.

Look at your calendar and choose one day soon when you can commit to acting on your messages for that entire day. Go easy on yourself and choose a day when commitments are minimal and when you'll have more time for yourself.

2. Begin your day in activation.

When the day arrives, begin by activating your Line. As you sit in activation, ask your Highest Self for support in remaining open to your messages and help with overcoming your doubt so you can trust your instinct when you've received a message. Sit in activation for as long as you want, thinking about the day ahead and bringing into your awareness any possible times when you think you'll feel tempted by energy that will pull you out of alignment and away from your messages.

As you sit in activation, ask your Highest Self the following questions:

What is one change to a habit, pattern, or routine I can make today?

What is one new thing I can do today?

What is something I've been putting off that I can do today?

What is one way I can show myself love today?

What is one way I can trust myself today?

3. Write down your messages.

After each question, write down the messages you received before asking the next. Your messages can be simple, like "set an alarm for tomorrow morning," or they can relate to a change you've wanted to make in your life. Whatever the message is, don't analyze it or expand on it; simply write it down as you received it.

4. Take action.

Of all the messages you receive, I want you to take action on three of them. A sense of accomplishment can be incredibly motivating, so choose the messages you're most comfortable acting on that day. I want you to feel what it's like to receive a message and follow through on it, and how consistently doing this makes it easier to overcome doubt, to accept that you don't have to know why you're receiving it or where it will lead, and to learn how to focus on yourself, not others. This may seem like a simple exercise, but a daily practice of acting on your messages is transformational.

5. Journal.

At the end of the day, answer the following journal prompts:

Acting on my messages made me feel . . .

One change I saw in my day from acting on a message was . . .

In the future, I can act on my messages by . . .

Taking action on your messages doesn't mean you're moving mountains in your life every day. It's usually the opposite. Your messages are like gentle whispers that show you the small changes you can make so it's easier for you to stay in alignment throughout your day. These subtle and consistent daily shifts are what will create the biggest impact in your life. Growth is a gradual process, and your messages will guide you every step of the way.

CHAPTER 5

LOVE IS THE THREAD THAT KEEPS YOU TOGETHER

DO YOU WANT TO SHINE? DO YOU WANT TO SHINE
THAT LOVE WITHIN YOU? IT IS SO EASY FOR YOU TO
DO, FOR IT IS SEWN RIGHT THROUGH YOU. ALL YOU
NEED TO DO IS ALLOW YOURSELF TO FEEL IT, SEE IT,
RELEASE IT, RECEIVE IT. THAT RAINBOW OF LOVE IS
WITHIN YOU, ALL AROUND YOU. GIVE IT AWAY, GIVE
IT AWAY, GIVE IT AWAY AS FREELY AND EASILY AS
MOTHER NATURE GIVES IT TO YOU EVERY DAY.

— THE PINNACLE

You are made of love. The energy within the realm of the Akashic Records, the energy of your messages, and the energy of your Line is love. Non-judgmental, unconditional, divine love. The Pinnacle have said that love is the only emotion on the other side of this human experience. It's why your messages are infused with love and why acting on a message is acting out of love for yourself. The most important thing we can learn in this physical life, according to the Pinnacle, is how to show ourselves this unconditional love. In every experience you have, every decision you make, and every emotion you feel, the love you're receiving through your Line will give you the strength and encouragement to accept yourself—for who you are, for your mental and emotional health, for what your physical body looks like, and for the experiences you have in this stage of your soul journey.

Love is something we're all capable of giving and receiving. It's something we all look for in life, whether from a partner, a parent, or a friend. But the love running through your Line is different from the love we know in this physical realm. This is love from God, the Universal One, Source Energy, or Creator. This love is divine. It's constantly flowing through you, and nothing you do will ever stop it. Just like your messages, it's up to you to receive it, understand what it feels like to you, and follow the guidance through your Line on how you can show it to yourself right now.

Even though this love is running through you, you need to make an active decision in every moment to show it to yourself. You're receiving messages right now on simple but effective ways you can love yourself. Are you open to receiving them?

This isn't always easy. Everyone has, at some point in their lives, failed to show themselves love. And even if you love yourself most of the time, you can probably remember a time when you didn't. Your ego may tell you that you're not worthy of love, or it may try to talk you out of changing the things you do that don't reflect this love. It may tell you that it isn't real and won't change how you feel.

But your ego is wrong. This love can lift you up when you're feeling low. It can pick you up when you've fallen over. It can sustain you when you feel depleted. This love will always be there for you to receive. Give yourself permission to accept it.

As the Pinnacle have said, "Allow yourself to feel it, see it, release it, receive it. And when you do, give it freely." Give this love freely to yourself and to your family, partner, kids, friends, coworkers, neighbors, and strangers. You give this love when you seek to understand rather than judge, when you find common ground instead of drawing a dividing line, when you understand your triggers before reacting, when you learn how to listen. When you use your messages to show yourself this love, you're better able to treat others around you with love, understanding, and compassion.

YOUR BODY NEEDS THIS LOVE

Your physical body needs the energy of this love. When it's not getting it, you will feel it, possibly as lethargy, melancholy, listlessness, depression, or an emptiness inside of you. There have been many periods in Ben's adult life where he has moved through severe episodes of depression. There were different life events that brought this energy on, but the common thread among them was that these were all times when he didn't feel like he knew how to love himself. On the outside, he looked healthy. He took care of his physical appearance and hygiene. He exercised and socialized. But inside there was a void.

With varying combinations of antidepressant medication, therapy, meditation, sitting in activation, and prayer, he learned how to accept himself for everything that made him who he is, including the energy of depression he was feeling, and love himself for it because this energy was pushing him to learn more about himself and grow stronger from it.

Sometimes what he needed was to show his true self to family and friends. Other times, he was guided to change habits that pulled him out of alignment, start new creative projects, or relearn how to live with awareness for each present moment. His messages always gave him tips on how he could reflect the love running through him in his life. This love didn't "cure" his depression; it was the catalyst, the boost he needed to pick himself up and learn how to manage the energy he was moving through.

When you activate your Line, you're opening yourself up to receiving a restorative energy your physical body craves. This love can help you feel energetically aligned and aware of the messages telling you how you can lift yourself back up. You are made of love, and this love is flowing through your Line every second of every day. This love will revive you, nourish you, and guide you.

The Pinnacle have taught me that "love is the thread that keeps you together. Even when you feel as though you're falling apart, it is the love that keeps you together. It is your Line; it is your love; it is your life force."

Before I guide you further on this journey back to yourself, I want you to learn how you can love every part of yourself: your soul, the multidimensional essence of you; your past, and every choice you've made that has brought you to this moment; and your physical body, the sacred container and home of your energy.

EXERCISE HEART ACTIVATION

It's time to activate your heart. The Pinnacle have shared with me that in order to open your heart to feel more love for yourself and others, the first thing you need to do is ask for it. This simple and profound exercise will shift something within you. You may feel it immediately or you may not. If not, give it time because you will feel it eventually.

By using your voice to ask for this love, you're activating a new love frequency within you. It can feel incredibly vulnerable to say something out loud instead of silently in your head, even if you're all alone and no one else is around. If this isn't something you're used to doing, you may feel uncomfortable or even exposed by doing this. I assure you that many in our community have felt the same way going through this exercise. Those same people have also said how transformational it is.

When you ask for more love, you will receive it. By opening your heart up for more love, you are also opening yourself up to the contrast and the lessons that also live within you, the opportunities for your soul to grow and evolve. Still, when you accept yourself your whole self, your full self, your soul-self—you can accept other people for who they are and hold more space for them. But, most importantly, you look for ways to see life through a lens of love. You see the world through love.

Begin by holding your hands up and out in front of you. Then, say the following words out loud: "I activate this love within me. I receive this love, I want this love, bring this love to me. I am ready for this love."

It's important to use your voice when reciting this. Your voice is very powerful. There are soundwaves within every word you speak and the vibration of these words can be received at a significant distance.

If you're not physically able to speak, then use your intention to invoke this love within you. It's important to note that you're not asking for this love from an external source. This love lives within you. By using your voice to invite it in, you're opening yourself up to align with its frequency.

LOVE YOUR JOURNEY

We all have something about us that we find hard to accept or wish we could change. At some point, maybe you've thought that if you had someone else's personality, talents, or upbringing you would be happier, or it would be easier to achieve your goals. As you uncover your many layers, remember that each one is part of your soul's essence. Without it, you wouldn't be you. You are made from stardust and each speck of you is intentional—there are no accidents.

You are not here to live someone else's life. When you look outside of yourself, you're not able to see the many ways you can receive the divine love flowing through you as limitless medicine. You're not able to see the gifts that light you up and shine your beauty onto the world. You're not able to learn the things your soul brought into this life for you to heal and evolve from. And you can't see the person your Highest Self is showing you that you are.

Loving yourself begins by accepting who you are. This life is a unique chapter in your soul journey. It was designed specifically for you. Yet it can be difficult to accept everything that makes you unique—your gifts, your trauma, your growth. Your messages can give you the reasons for every experience you've had and every emotional reaction you feel, but to arrive at a complete understanding, you must see everything you go through within the context of this life and your soul journey and not how it compares to someone else's. When you can do this, you are accepting who you are and showing yourself the love you deserve.

When you compare yourself to others or try to live your life according to someone else's standards, you will be pulled out of alignment, which will make it more challenging to receive your messages. You'll doubt your guidance. Or, instead of realizing how you're being guided to respond, you'll wonder how someone else would react. You'll wish for a different life and not see how your messages are leading you to one where you're fully loving yourself and showing your true self to the world.

When you're moving through difficult moments, it can be tempting to think that things are much easier for everyone else but you, that life is out to get you, or that you're being punished by God or the Universe. These are all things I've heard from members of our community. As I tell them, it's just as easy to shift your energy to a more aligned state as it is to feed this low vibrational energy, but it may seem difficult if you're not used to doing it. Activating your Line is the quickest way to step out of the energy of envy, resentment, or jealousy that comparison feeds.

You are always in control of your energy, and it only takes a few minutes to realign with your Highest Self, but you must train yourself to make this your new default response to low vibrational situations. By doing a Line Activation, you're not only pulling yourself out of this low vibrational state, you're also opening yourself up to learning why you compare yourself to others and receiving practical ways you can stop it. A member in our community shared with me that her daily Line Activation practice brings her into stillness so she can sit with herself and "face all the uncomfortable stuff" because all of the distractions of trying to fix her external world are removed and her focus is placed on her internal world. The organic unfolding of being in stillness invited in more clarity, more self-realization, more self-worth, and more love. "You're connecting to all of your energy, which is made up of love. It's all love," she said.

Living a life in the Line will not only make it easier to stop yourself from making unhealthy comparisons, but it will also support you in shifting your focus back to you and your energy so you can see yourself in all your divine beauty. It will make it easier to remember the things you love about yourself, because there *are* things you do love about yourself, even if they're subtle and small. Sometimes you just need to be reminded of them.

EXERCISE YOUR LIST OF LOVE

Listing everything you love about yourself is a simple yet intimate exercise that will help you see, remember, or deepen the love you have for yourself. During this process, you may have heart-opening realizations, you may feel frustrated or sad, you may feel gratitude, or you may feel nothing at all. Honor every emotion you feel because each one is bringing you closer to your love.

1. Activate your Line.

Begin by doing a Line Activation. Imagine that the energy flowing through you is like water, gently cleansing any resistance you hold within your heart that makes it difficult for you to accept your own love.

2. Sit in activation.

As you sit in activation, continue to invite this love into your awareness. Focus entirely on yourself and your love. If distracting thoughts or emotions come in, acknowledge them, then release them and focus back on the love you hold for yourself. You can also release a few deep exhales if you feel it supports you in letting go of any stuck energy, like feelings of shame, worthlessness, or fear.

If you need help feeling this love, remember that the palms of your hands are energetically connected to your heart. If it's comfortable for you, hold your hands over your heart or hold your hands up and out, with your palms open, to allow the love to flow through you.

3. Journal.

When you're ready, create a list of at least five things you love about yourself. These can be small, simple things or big things. Honor what's coming through from your Highest Self; this is divine guidance.

Your insecurities may try to hide all the beautiful qualities you genuinely love about yourself, but remember that this is your ego trying to keep you in old patterns by preventing you from exploring a new way of loving yourself. If this is happening for you, neutrally acknowledge your ego's plan and then, as if you're politely asking a friend to leave, dismiss your ego by saying out loud, "It's time for you to leave."

If you've listed your five things and still have more, continue writing until you feel you're finished.

4. Recite your love.

When you've finished your list, stand in front of a mirror, look into your eyes, and begin reciting everything you love about yourself. Go through your entire list, point by point, expressing this love to yourself. You may immediately feel emotionally moved by this experience, or you may have to repeat it several times to receive the love you're gifting to yourself. Repeat this exercise as many times as you need to until you deeply feel what you are saying.

Optional: If you could benefit from daily reminders of the love you hold for yourself, do a Line Activation every morning and as you sit in activation, ask for a self-love mantra to use for that day. Whenever you feel like you're not showing yourself love or need a reminder of the love within you, find a mirror and recite it while looking yourself in the eye. Look deeply into your eyes as you speak, as if you're peering into your soul, and hold this focus for a few moments after as well. Feel this love flow through your body, opening your heart, and softening yourself to its healing power.

LOVE YOUR PAST

Everyone has a past. And in everyone's past, there are moments we wish we had handled differently. There are words we said or didn't say and things we did or didn't do that, in hindsight, we would've done differently. I used to spend a lot of time and energy focusing on these moments. I would allow myself to be pulled away from love by shame, telling myself I should've known better. I often wished I could repeat a situation because I wanted to prove to myself that I was better than how I acted. Of course, this wasn't possible, and knowing I couldn't change the past made me feel stuck, like I was trying to peddle a bike through a muddy field—spinning my tires but not moving forward.

Loving yourself means seeing how every moment of your life is a connected and important part of your soul's evolution. It's common to try to learn from the "mistakes" in your past and play the situation over and over in your mind, but there's a difference between learning from your past and reliving the energy of these experiences. You'll know you're reliving the energy when you immediately feel the emotion (shame, guilt, regret, or embarrassment) from that experience. When you do this without learning from the situation, you're not loving yourself; you're punishing yourself. The Pinnacle have said, "Guilt does not fix a situation; it does not make anyone feel better. Guilt, in fact, only poisons you."

Imagine everything in your past, especially those memories that bring up emotions like shame, guilt, or remorse, as your breath. Every breath is a breath already breathed. Exhale and let them go, creating more space within your physical body to receive the love flowing within you.

The reason we feel such a wide range of emotions is because we learn different things from each of them. When you feel consumed by your emotional reactions to a past situation, you still have a choice. You can allow yourself to be pulled out of the present moment and feel stuck in the past that you're unable to change, or remain in the present where you can use your Line and your messages to tell yourself a new story about your past.

EXERCISE THE NEW STORY OF YOU

If you find that you're often reliving the emotions of your past experiences instead of learning from them, this exercise will help you tell yourself a different story about your past, one infused with love, so you can receive what you've learned and see how you've grown.

1. Activate your Line.

Begin by doing a Line Activation, and as you sit in activation, imagine a surge of loving energy flow through your Line. You are made of this love. You are this love.

2. Journal.

Think of an experience in your past through which you had trouble showing yourself love and reflect on how you grew from it. Use the following prompts to write about this experience:

Describe the experience by writing what happened and with whom, where, and when it happened.

What feelings come up now when you think about it?

Now, think of something you learned from this experience and how it contributed to your growth or prepared you for something to come. Use the following prompt to guide your writing:

I can show myself love for this experience because . . .

When you're not showing yourself love, you aren't able to see how everything you've experienced has been for your higher learning and growth. You can create a complete story of your past that reflects love for who you are and everything you've gone through, and this story is always yours to tell.

LOVE YOUR CONTAINER

The Pinnacle have said that as your energy changes, your body changes as well. Throughout my pregnancy, I practiced prenatal yoga twice a week. One of the instructors would often refer to our bodies as a "container" for the baby and said that this container was changing throughout our pregnancies to support new life. Accepting these changes would help us to find comfort (surrender) in the discomfort (labor).

This was a profound teaching that helped me cultivate a new relationship with my body so I could accept and embrace every way it needed to change and move, surrendering with full trust to the process. In my spiritual practice, I took this analogy further. Not only was my body a container for my baby, it was also a container for my soul and, for that brief moment in time, my daughter's soul as well. As soon as I began to look at my body as a physical container for my soul, I was able to love it for the energy it carries.

Your body is a physical incarnation of your energy, and as you move through life, your body is going to change as your energy changes. When you're carrying the energy of heavy emotions, you may feel heavy as well. You may feel weak, lethargic, overly full (even if you haven't eaten much food), or constantly exhausted. You may have a headache or experience inflammation or pain somewhere within your body. After you've done the work to release this energy, you may feel a lot lighter, more nimble, and maybe even stronger. This is not about how your body looks from the outside but about how you energetically experience your body from within—how it feels to be in your skin.

Receiving your body as a physical container for your soul supports you in honoring what a miraculous gift it is to live within it. Your soul chose this body as its home, and it's a divine gift to be carried within it every single day. The way you speak about yourself and your physical body will impact the way you feel about it. Even if you feel disconnected from your body right now, or perhaps you're not even inspired to take care of it, practicing gratitude for your body can shift your energy and support you in receiving it as a divine home for your soul. Give thanks to your physical container and honor it as your temple for carrying your energy throughout this human experience.

As with many things, when it comes to deepening your love and connection with your physical body, Earth Activations can support you. Go into nature, jump into the sea, hug a tree, or sit outside on the ground with profound awareness of everything around you and do a Line Activation. Our community members have shared with us that when they practice a Line Activation close to Mother Earth's energy, they have felt instant relief from physical symptoms of anxiety, a tight jaw, an unsettled stomach, aches, or overall tension. Every Earth Activation you experience can also be a reminder to love your physical container because there's so much more than what you see.

GROW INTO YOUR LOVE

The Pinnacle have said, "The heart is meant to expand. It is meant to grow. It is meant to be filled up like a balloon, so it can support you in rising. What happens when you let go of a helium balloon? It floats up. Your heart within you is like a helium balloon, and as it continues to expand, it elevates you."

Loving yourself is a journey. You will have times when your self-love carries you through the ups and downs of life, and you will also have times when you feed energy that makes it harder to see your love. But remember, this love is here for you. You don't need to look for it; it's within you. Make it a daily practice to open yourself up to it. Open your heart and your awareness to the transcendent love that lives within you.

No matter where you are at on your soul journey, loving yourself begins with accepting yourself as you are in this very moment—flying high or feeling stuck or trapped in whatever life situation you're currently in. Honestly accept everything that brought you to this moment and then release it. Give yourself space and time to adjust to the energy of this love, especially if it is new to you.

Your energy is constantly flowing, moving, and evolving, and therefore the ways you love yourself will change along with it. Openly receive what's coming through your Line on how to love yourself right now, and then show yourself grace and compassion as you process it. There is no deadline or time frame for when you need to have this all figured out. Trust and surrender to your journey; this is loving yourself.

When you're showing yourself love, it will radiate around you and impact everything you do. It will positively touch everyone you come in contact with and enrich your relationships. But the reason the Pinnacle have said that loving yourself is one of your main purposes is because you must learn to show yourself this love first before you can show it to others.

It is possible to love others without loving yourself, but the love you share with them will not reflect the divine love that is flowing through you. Over time, it may exhaust you, it may make your relationships unbalanced, or it may leave you feeling unfulfilled. When you learn what it feels like to receive this love for yourself, you'll be more open to understanding the messages you're receiving on how you can show it to others in your life.

In the next part of this book, you will begin the deep inner work of finding your way back to yourself. You will be confronting your actions, habits, and patterns that you've been ignoring or not seeing and learning how your messages are showing you a new way to live. Whenever you're engaged in this kind of self-reflection, it's important that you set the intention of doing it out of love for yourself. Remember, love is the thread that keeps you together, and you can do anything when it's done from a place of love.

CHAPTER 6

CREATING SPACE FOR SOUL GROWTH

IT MAY FEEL LIKE THINGS ARE CHANGING AND SHIFTING.
LIKE YOU ARE EXPERIENCING A ROLLOVER OF EVENTS,
A ROLLOVER OF ENERGY, A ROLLOVER OF EVERYTHING
THAT YOU KNEW, ALMOST AS IF WHAT ONCE WAS CAN
NO LONGER BE AND SO RIGHT NOW YOU'RE MOVING
THROUGH THE MOTION OF THE ROLLOVER. AND THIS IS
EXACTLY DIVINELY PLANNED YOU SEE, THIS IS EXACTLY
HOW YOUR SOUL WANTED IT TO BE. EVERYTHING
IS NEW AND EVERYTHING IS FRESH, AS IF BRAND
NEW FLOWERS ARE TAKING THEIR FIRST BREATH.

- THE PINNACLE

Your soul needs space in your life to move, change, grow, and evolve. You can regularly give your soul this space by practicing daily Line Activations and sitting in activation to feel the energy of your Line, receive your messages, and learn what you can do that day to live in alignment with your Highest Self. When you finish your Line Activation and open your eyes, you return to your physical life where you need to learn how to navigate the energy of your daily life from a place of alignment.

Everything you do, say, and think has an underlying energetic frequency. Like all frequencies, you'll feel this in your physical body as a particular emotion or sensation. In your energetic body, it's a little different. The frequencies underlying your actions either support you or they pull you out of alignment with your Line. Your emotions provide helpful clues to how you're feeling in your energetic body at a particular moment: are your actions aligned with the divine love flowing through you, or not? A regular day consists of hundreds of big and small actions, and the frequency you're feeling in your energetic body will change as a result. One of the reasons why the Pinnacle shared the Line Activation practice is to give you a clear way of shifting your frequency back into alignment when it inevitably moves out of alignment.

Your frequency is also constantly changing because you are a sponge that absorb energy from anywhere: the online content you consume, the shows you watch, the news you read, the "mood" of a room, and the conversations you have. Whenever you give your attention to something, you're opening yourself up to receiving an energetic frequency, and this will in turn affect your frequency—how you feel emotions in your physical body and whether you feel in alignment in your energetic body. You can read a news article written to provoke your fear and feel afraid, or you can watch a sad movie and feel empathy. This can happen without you being aware of the change in your emotions.

We are all affected by the energy we consume, and we require an intentional shift in our awareness to spot the habits or patterns that are pulling us out of alignment. I once read for a client who was experiencing a lot of anxiety, fatigue, and fear. In our reading, the Pinnacle suggested that a simple change in her evening routine would help. She would often watch a crime show before going to bed, and the Pinnacle said that the energy of these shows, which contain plots that often feed fear and anxiety, was preventing her from enjoying a restful sleep. They suggested that if she wanted to watch something at night, she should find a show with energy that matched the emotions she wanted to feel before going to bed in order to sleep better. She wasn't aware of the effect these shows had on her physical and energetic bodies. Making this connection was so empowering for her because with a simple switch, she could feel much better emotionally and create a new routine that was in alignment for her. The same is true for you: the moment you begin to discover where your energy is going and how it's affecting you, you're taking back your control and learning what you need to do to live an aligned life.

CLEAR THE CLUTTER

There are many things that can pull you out of alignment, and these will differ from person to person, but generally these will be things that take your focus away from your energy (how you're feeling in that moment, physically and energetically) and your Line (the frequency you can align with to change how you're feeling). Whatever is pulling you out of alignment, let's call it your energetic clutter. One of the biggest reasons why it can be difficult to receive your messages isn't from a lack of ability (trust me, you can do this); it's because the energetic clutter in your life is affecting your emotional state and making it harder for you to shift your energy into alignment and receive the guidance coming through your Line. In everything you do, you're bringing energy to it and consuming the energy from it. When you can make connections between what you do and how you feel from doing it, you'll be able to spot your energetic clutter and learn what you need to clear.

It's very common for the energetic clutter in your life to manifest into physical clutter in your home. This was the case for another former client of mine, specifically in her closet. In our reading, the Pinnacle pointed out a pattern of hers that she was unaware of. Whenever she would look for something to wear, she would immediately feel overwhelmed by everything in front of her and close the doors in frustration and defeat. She went through this many times throughout the day, every single day, but didn't see it as a sign of anything. To her, it was like an automatic response that had been happening for years: open the closet, feel frustrated, close the closet, feel defeated. Although she didn't enjoy feeling like this, it wasn't a surprise to her because it had become her normal. Her ego had been keeping her safe by repeating what was familiar, so she didn't question it.

When the Pinnacle brought this up, she laughed and said that every time she had gotten into her car for the past few weeks, she had received a message to drive to a bookstore to buy a book about tidying up her life. She knew she needed to sort through her cluttered closet but had yet to do something about it. Even though she had received guidance from her Highest Self on how to shift her experience, she was in a pattern that was uncomfortable yet safe, and so it continued to play out, day after day. Through our reading, she realized how connected she really was to her messages even though she felt unorganized in her life.

It can be this easy to make these connections because it only takes a split second of alignment to your Line's frequency to receive your messages. When you receive a message, you may feel like you're being reminded of something you already know, feel, or believe deep within yourself. You then make a choice, whether you're aware of it or not, to acknowledge and follow through on the message or ignore it altogether. You're receiving these little confirmations all the time. Maybe in the past you've shrugged them off, thinking, "Yes, I know I need to do that," but you don't follow through because you feel you don't have the time, your focus is pulled away by something else, or you don't think it's important. Your soul wants to guide you, but you have to turn on your awareness to your energy so you can see that you have the time, that you can clear the energetic clutter that's getting in between you and your messages, and that your messages are divine guidance to help you make positive changes in your life. Every single one, even the small and seemingly inconsequential ones, are important.

Imagine your energy is water from a faucet. Every time you give your attention to something (a conversation, a thought, a post on social media, etc.), you are turning on a faucet and letting your energy run. You are doing this in every moment of your day, and depending on how you manage your energy, you may have several faucets running at all times, long after you turned them on. You can be irritated by a conversation with someone in the morning and when night falls, you're still thinking about it. Or you could be angered by something you saw online and two days later you're still feeding that frequency, allowing that emotion to grow within you. The pattern of things you do, say, or think (such as a comfortable routine, the habits you use as a distraction from your feelings, assumptions you regularly make about others, etc.) can put you in situations that make you feel anxious, stressed, resentful, fatigued, lethargic, or hopeless. These faucets can leave you feeling like you're carrying a lot of energetic weight and have little time, strength, or focus left for yourself.

You can use your Line to identify which faucets are on and learn how to see the energetic effect they have on you. If it seems overwhelming to make these connections, I suggest looking at the things you do in your free time. There are a lot of easy and entertaining ways to distract yourself, and the way you spend your free time can help you understand whether you're numbing yourself to how you feel emotionally and energetically or intentionally doing things that support your alignment. Your clutter can be the things you do in your free time without any intention other than to subconsciously numb or switch off. During this time, you have an opportunity to make small changes in your life that will help you stay switched on to your messages and your energy.

In many client readings, the Pinnacle would bring up eating habits as one way to learn how to make intentional choices that align with what you need in that moment. When you're hungry, do you choose something that will support you physically and energetically, or something that will move slowly—and sometimes painfully—within you and your energy? In other words, do you eat food that will make you feel energized and balanced, or bloated and lethargic? When you eat intuitively, you open yourself up to the guidance you're receiving in that moment on what food will be most supportive to you. Here's how to do it: Before choosing something to eat, close your eyes and imagine the Line running through you. Take a few deep breaths and ask, "What will nourish my body in this moment?" Be open to receiving anything that's coming through to you. Sometimes, you'll receive a message saying you're not actually hungry but either bored or looking for a distraction. Other times, you may be guided to eat a smaller portion than you usually have, food that you've never tried before, or an entirely new eating schedule. Eating intuitively means being responsive to the changing needs of your physical and energetic self.

The Pinnacle have also suggested to many of my former clients to use their fridge as an exercise in clearing energetic clutter. When you open your fridge, what do you see? Do you have food that will bring you energy and vitality or food that will sit heavily within you? You can clean the clutter of your fridge by clearing food that's expired, unhealthy, or unsupportive to what your messages are telling you that you need. The lessons you learn from this experience will directly translate to the clutter in other areas of your life, and you can practice paying attention to your messages in these areas as well. You can also practice intuitive reading by opening yourself up to a book, magazine, or topic you're feeling called to read. Intuitive walking can simply be heading out the door with no set destination and being open to being guided on your journey. The key to any of these activities is to learn how to spot when your ego is trying to keep you safe by repeating familiar patterns or habits and trusting that your messages will open you up to new experiences and new understandings of yourself.

EXERCISE CLEAR YOUR CLUTTER

Think back to a time you recently spent all by yourself that, by the end, you wished you had spent differently. Perhaps you had something you wanted to accomplish, but you kept getting distracted by mindlessly scrolling social media. Or maybe you wanted to spend the night at home, and you fought your exhaustion to go out to a social obligation. However you spent the time, it was not what you knew deep within you (or confirmed by your messages) that you should have done.

When you've thought of a time, use the following journal prompts to help you make connections between what you did and how it made you feel.

How did you spend your time?

Did you feel or receive any messages at any point (before, during, or after) that you should do something else?

How did you feel, emotionally and/or energetically, during and after?

Is there something you did that you think might be energetic clutter that you need to clear? This can mean eliminating that activity, reducing how often you do it, or being intentional with when you do it and for how long. Your clutter can make you feel energetically low, so review what you wrote for the third journal prompt; this will be your first clue in identifying your clutter.

PRIORITIZE YOURSELF

Clearing your energetic clutter helps you see what's not supporting your alignment, but not everything that's pulling you out of alignment is something you can or want to get rid of. One of the most beautiful aspects of life is the variety of relationships we build with each other as spouses, partners, friends, children, parents, siblings, coworkers, classmates, and so on. There will be times in every one of your relationships where the energy you're giving or receiving makes you feel like you don't have the clarity or space to align with yourself and receive your messages. Just like with your energetic clutter, you can use your Line to learn the changes you need to make so you feel like you're prioritizing yourself, your messages, and your alignment while fully participating in your relationships.

When you're prioritizing yourself, you're living with an awareness of the energy you're giving to and receiving from people in your life. You know your intention for every faucet you have on so you can manage and act from a place of alignment with yourself and the love running through you. We are all connected by the energy that flows through every one of us and when you feed these connections with divine love, this energy grows on micro and macro levels and ripples throughout the world. When you know why you're giving your energy to someone and are aware that you also have the power to turn that faucet off, you can stop yourself from feeling energetically drained, anxious, panicked, or lost when you're giving away too much of yourself. And you can change your actions and intentions to create meaningful and supportive exchanges with those faucets you choose to turn on.

Relationships are a series of energetic exchanges. You give your energy to someone, and you receive energy from them in return. The energetic exchanges we share with each other are an essential part of this beautiful experience, and the love we can give and receive in our relationships enriches our lives in a way nothing else can. But in every relationship you will experience a contrast of high and low emotions. There will be moments when you feel you're receiving exactly the energy you need, and other times when you will feel pulled out of alignment by something that was said or done.

Sometimes it will be a type of exchange (gossip, resentment, or even your attempts to convince someone that you're right) that you need to change.

Other times you may need to turn off a relationship faucet for a brief period of time, or maybe permanently. Use the nonjudgmental, divine love flowing through your Line to help you become aware of how your faucets are impacting you on an energetic level. This will help you break free from the unsupportive patterns your ego wants you to continue, so you can see your relationships in terms of learning and growth. You must also take responsibility for your actions and understand the energy you're bringing to your relationships. This will help you see the changes that can be made to improve the relationship, or when it's time for a relationship to change or end.

There are some relationships in which your faucet is on only when you're interacting with them. With coworkers, for example, the end of a working day can help you subconsciously turn the faucet off. If you find that the faucet is still running, think specifically about the energy underneath the interactions by understanding what emotions you're still giving them. Was something said or did something happen that triggered your emotions? When you want to shift your frequency, do a Line Activation and ask your Highest Self for clarity to learn why this faucet is still running and how you can turn it off. This puts your focus back on you and your energy, so you can learn how to respond from a place of alignment. If you need to speak your truth, if you need to release, or if you need to offer support, your messages will guide you to your next step.

With friends and family, the relationship faucets are usually always running, at least a little bit. Prioritizing your energy doesn't mean putting yourself and your needs above everyone else, all the time. Children, for example, are a big energy faucet—the tap can feel like it's always wide open. There can be major ups and downs and very often parents ride that wave of emotion along with their children. Energy management, even in these situations, starts with awareness. How are you feeling that day (what energy are you bringing to the interactions)? What does an aligned response to a tantrum look like for you and your child (how can you put aside what you're feeling and look for opportunities for learning and growth)? What are the larger energetic reasons for conflict between you and your child (what are you moving through in your life that is affecting how you show up in the relationship)? There will still be friction, especially for children, because growth can be uncomfortable, but the more aware of your energy you are (this applies to all relationships), the easier it is to spot the many ways you can be pulled out of alignment before it happens.

When you give your energy to so many things, it can often feel like your emotions are dictated by everything else in your life except you. Yet this is *your* life. When you look at all your energy faucets from the perspective of your love, growth, and evolution, you can decide which ones stay on, where you can make changes to improve others, and which ones you need to turn off. But to do this, you need to first be aware of where your energy is going and what kind of energy you're receiving in return. This awareness is developed by learning acceptance, release, and gratitude for every difficult moment, because each one is helping you know yourself a little better.

EXERCISE ENERGY FAUCETS

Think of a time you were giving your energy to someone when you weren't physically with them or talking to them. You may have done so earlier that day or week, but the moment I want you to think of is when you were giving them your energy by thinking about them or feeling an emotional reaction to them or a situation involving them. And the more energy of yours that you gave, the lower you felt, energetically and emotionally. Then use the following journal prompts to write about your experience:

Why were you thinking of this person or feeling an emotion about them? Did a hurtful memory come up, was something said or done, were you doing something that reminded you of that person?

What did you do in that moment to feed the energy or emotion and keep your faucet on? Did you replay a conversation over and over in your mind, did you gossip with someone about them, did you belittle yourself and your worth?

What could you have done to shift your energy or emotion? Focus on simple, practical actions, like going for a walk or run, speaking your truth to that person, or releasing old feelings. If you need support, activate your Line and ask your Highest Self for guidance.

If you notice that you are regularly feeling energetically low within a certain relationship, I suggest thinking of changes you can make that put you at the front of the line. You can start by saying no to things you don't want to do or to topics you don't want to discuss that aren't in alignment with what you need in that moment. By saying no, you're establishing boundaries that put you and your energy first. Start with something small to help build your confidence and be gentle with yourself during this process.

STRETCHING TIME

When you make decisions that align with your messages, you are allowing yourself to be led by your soul. The more often you show up as this version of yourself, the more you'll discover other ways you can put yourself at the front of the line in your life. Unfollow the accounts on social media that cause you to feel triggered, jealous, insecure, guilty, or upset, turn off the news sources that feed frequencies that pull you out of alignment, and limit your online engagement so you can do things that bring you back home to yourself, like spending time in nature, taking up a new hobby or returning to an old one, or simply breaking out of routines that are numbing you from the miraculous beauty of this life. You may want to end a relationship or rediscover your partner by intentionally creating time to talk to each other, with no screens allowed.

There will be high and low energetic moments throughout your day and over the course of your life. As you continue to develop your awareness of the energy of each situation, it will become easier to learn the reasons for your feelings. Knowing the energy you're feeding in these moments will help you learn how to move through them without being overcome by whatever it is you're feeling. The more aware you become of where your energy is going, the more time you'll feel you have for yourself, your soul, and your growth.

Your messages will keep coming and you need to give yourself the time to receive them and act on them. This isn't always easy. Days are busy and move quickly, and the responsibilities you have to the people in your life make it hard to ensure you're still making time for yourself. On a busy day, how do you spend the moments you have to yourself? Rather than giving your energy away to social media, emails, news, or texts, you can stretch the time you do have by focusing on your breath, your heartbeat, the energy flowing through your body, and the present moment you're in. Go outside, even if just for a moment, and connect with your Earth Activation Point. Close your eyes and breathe in the fresh air, feeling your lungs expand and contract with each breath. Imagine your inhales and exhales to last minutes rather than seconds. This simple practice will rejuvenate you and reconnect you back to yourself because it feels like an energetic refreshment.

Within every minute, there is an opportunity to bring your energy back to yourself. You can break out of the habits that needlessly give it away by doing a Line Activation instead. Return to your energetic home, your place of connection, and ask for clarity on what you're looking to distract yourself from. The messages coming through your Line gently and lovingly provide enormous clarity on your emotional state and the energetic reasons for your feelings. When you are intentional with how you spend your time, are regularly clearing your energetic clutter, and are aware of your energetic faucets, even a busy day can feel calm and well-paced and provide enough energy to focus on yourself and your growth.

CHAPTER 7

THE ENERGETIC CONTRAST OF YOUR TRANSFORMATION

YOU'RE BEAUTIFUL WHEN YOU'RE ALL LIT UP. THIS LIGHT
COMES FROM WITHIN. IT GLOWS THROUGH YOUR EYES,
YOUR SKIN, YOUR ENERGY, AND IT GLOWS THROUGH YOUR
SMILE. THIS DOESN'T MEAN YOU'RE HAPPY ALL THE
TIME. THIS MEANS YOU HAVE CONNECTION. YOU FEEL
YOUR LOVE AND YOU'RE CONNECTED TO IT. YOU HONOR
IT, YOU GIVE IT COMPASSION, YOU GIVE IT GRATITUDE,
AND YOU GIVE IT SERVICE. YOU GIVE YOURSELF SERVICE.

- THE PINNACLE

Energy is always moving, and your experiences are always changing. If you're someone who tries new things and enjoys being in unfamiliar situations, you'll see this reflected in your own life. But even if you crave consistency and routine, and every day of your life is like the one before, you're still experiencing change. On a physical cellular level, your body is repairing, regenerating, and aging every minute of every day. Your energy doesn't stand still either.

In the previous chapter you looked at the energetic ups and downs of your day-to-day life. You may have noticed that even if your day was relatively calm, your energy still fluctuated. If you took the opportunity to make space in your life by clearing away the energetic clutter, you may have found yourself in new experiences and moving through new energy. Any time you do something new, like change a routine, break a habit, or follow through on a message, you'll take on new or different energy, both high and low. It's the low vibrational energy that can be the most confusing and even disheartening, but I invite you to embrace all forms of energy as a transformative gift. In this life, you learn from the contrasting energy of every experience. It's how you grow, change, and transform.

THE PATTERN OF ENERGY

The Pinnacle have said the energy you experience in life moves in waves of high and low frequencies. Some highs will be higher than others and some lows will be lower than others, but the pattern will remain consistent: a high vibrational energy will be followed by a low vibrational energy, followed by another high vibrational energy, followed by another low vibrational energy, and on and on. Some highs feel really good, while others can feel positive but not outstanding. It's the same for low waves. A low vibrational energy can feel really challenging and difficult to move through, or it can feel moderate and manageable. It's all relative to your ability to manage energy as you move through the experience.

This energetic pattern can help you become aware of the energy to come but this doesn't mean you'll always know the specific circumstances that bring this energy to you. Sometimes you'll spot a clear connection to a recent decision you made or life event you're moving through. Other times, you'll feel a shift in your emotions but won't immediately know what caused the change. There's a sacred mystery in this gift of life and surrendering to it is part of this journey. We're not supposed to know what happens next and although trying to figure it out may be exciting, it will distract you from your messages that will support you through any energy you feel.

The Pinnacle have said, "There are so many things to come, you see, be patient my dear, your roots are like a tree. And roots take time to grow, to expand, and to reach; in time there will be so much you reach. So do not rush your time, be open to what comes and come back to 'me.'" What the Pinnacle mean by "coming back to 'me'" is returning yourself to the loving and supportive energy of your Line so you can feel, with confidence and connection, like you have everything within you to move through the challenging moments.

Imagine your physical body is the neck of a guitar and the energetic memories of all your soul experiences (your Akashic Records) are the strings. Every experience you have in this life is directly connected to at least one of these soul experiences. It's like a string is strummed and the emotions of that memory vibrate through your body as a high or low vibrational energy. The experience in your physical life that activated this soul memory is a clue to deeper soul learning. You may only receive small pieces of information at the time, but these individual pieces help you understand the larger energetic reasons for how you feel the energetic waves in your life. It can be challenging to work through the soul growth that this energy brings, but energy is always moving, so you can find comfort, relief, and strength in the fact that any difficult situation, whatever it is, won't last forever.

EMBRACE THE ENERGETIC CONTRAST

Your pattern of energy moves in waves of high and low vibrations, but this doesn't mean you'll only feel one of them at a time. In fact, it's very common to feel both high and low at the same time. Energy moves much faster than our physical bodies can keep up with and sometimes we can be physically processing the effects of the energy we've received long after it has passed. This can feel like fatigue, a tight jaw, indigestion, a headache, dizziness, or a racing heart, amongst many other physical expressions in which energetic waves can play out. At times, the energetic waves of emotion move in and out of your body very close together, making it even more challenging to physically navigate the energy within your body. For example, you'll have a high vibrational experience that's quickly followed by a low vibrational thought, feeling, or desire. You're processing the low energy while at the same time basking in the high energy.

When our community members are feeling this energetic contrast, they often feel like they need to choose the high vibrational feeling over the low. Worse, if they're overwhelmed by their sadness, anxiety, fear, or whatever they've labeled as "low," they feel guilty and worried that they're attracting more low vibrational energy into their life. Although we regularly use the terms high and low to describe the feelings associated with these energies, energy itself doesn't come with a label. We label energy to help us understand how we experience it in our body. But there is also an implicit judgment that usually comes along with it: low is "bad," high is "good."

As a soul moving through the human experience, you are designed to feel all emotions and process all energy. You are not wrong or weak for feeling low vibrational energy. You are not being punished by the Universe, Source, or God for having experiences that are bringing up challenging emotions. These judgments are thousands of years deep within our psyche, but we're being supported right now in releasing them and forming a new relationship with ourselves and our emotions. Every emotion you feel is designed for your soul's growth.

If you feed low vibrational energy rather than understanding why you're feeling it so you can move through it, you are not calling more of it in. But you will experience this energy for longer or with greater intensity, and sometimes this will happen when you're trying to work through difficult emotions and understand how your soul wants to grow through it. When you acknowledge these emotions rather than suppress them, you are not sending a signal to the Universe that you want more of this energy. You are gaining more awareness and insight about yourself, your responses, your lessons, and your soul's path. These lower vibrational energies also don't preclude you from entering your Akashic Records or using your Line. You can activate your Line and receive your messages in any emotional or energetic state. Your messages are here to help you through every situation you're in and every emotion you feel.

While it's true that high vibrational energy can feel emotionally "better" than low vibrational energy, they both play a part in your growth. Your high vibrational experiences can feel like confirmations from your soul that you're in alignment, but it's your low vibrational moments that teach you what alignment looks like to you. Choosing to only experience high vibrational emotions without learning from the low vibrational emotions is like embarking on a journey and changing course whenever the terrain gets rough, or the weather turns inclement. You may choose a thought, feeling, or activity that makes you feel the way you want, but if you don't know what you need to be in alignment you will always be chasing these high vibrational feelings without understanding where it is your soul is guiding you.

It's not the type of emotion you feel that matters most; it's how you respond. When you feel high vibrational emotions, do you know what you did that made you feel them? Were you responding to your messages? What does this tell you about the things your soul needs for your alignment? When you're experiencing low vibrational emotions, do you ignore them? Do you blame others for them? Do you feed them and allow them to grow? Or do you receive each one as an opportunity to go deeper within yourself?

Soul work is not always easy, but you make it harder for yourself when you are selective about what emotions you choose to acknowledge and learn from. This work can be uncomfortable. It can be sad. It can be painful. But on the other side is a greater awareness of yourself and what you need to be in alignment. It can be helpful to zoom out of the specific situation you're in and see the larger pattern of energy and the soul work it's connected to. The Pinnacle have said, "You must look at yourself from above, always. Do not only look within the 3D body; seek a multidimensional view by looking from above. You always want to look from above; this gives gratitude and perspective, and it allows you to see in love. The moment you feel within that 'this is all happening to me,' that's when victimhood begins. When you can see from above, you know within your heart that everything is happening for a brand-new start." Buried deep in every emotion, even pain, lies wisdom from your soul. Look from above, see with love, and receive every experience as an opportunity for growth and higher learning.

Alignment won't always feel good. Being in alignment means you're on your soul path and open to your emotions, growth, and healing. It doesn't mean bypassing low vibrational energy or experiences. You need these to grow; they are your teachers. When you avoid them out of fear, guilt, or your ego, you're keeping yourself from the full experience of being human, which is *feeling* all emotions. To emotionally feel is to heal. Your messages will guide you to uncomfortable experiences where you're dealing with low vibrational emotions. You may think you're out of alignment, but these experiences and emotions are where the learning happens. Don't shy away from them. This is where your soul grows and where you transform.

TRANSFORMATION BEGINS IN DISCOMFORT

When someone in our community is processing a sudden life change or navigating an uncomfortable experience (car accident, job loss, divorce, physical injury, etc.), they'll often write to me about their situation and ask, "Why is this happening to *me*?" As with everything in life that happens *to* us, there's the temptation of sitting in a low vibration and allowing it to grow rather than using the low vibrational energy as a catalyst to access the high vibrational energy of soul learning and healing. These challenging moments are opportunities to make significant changes in your life. When you accept that discomfort is part of your transformation, you are rewiring your brain to think "*Why* is this happening to me?" instead of "Why is this happening to *me*?"

In moments of physical or energetic discomfort are the seeds of transformation.

The Pinnacle have shared a beautiful metaphor to describe how transformation begins when you're uncomfortable: "You need to look at the Earth, how the plates move, how mountains are formed, how cracks begin and how holes, craters, and canyons are formed. We take lessons from the Earth. Allow the Earth to show you how to move and how to transform, for the Earth is a mirror to you. All these beautiful landscapes were formed from change. The Earth is always changing and so are you."

Open yourself to your discomfort without trying to find a shortcut through it or trying to mask yourself from your feelings. You are showing yourself love when you allow yourself to receive and embrace your emotions. At the same time, be mindful of how you're managing your energy. Do a Line Activation when you need to balance your low vibrational energy and remain aware of the messages showing you the high vibrational contrast of this experience: what you can learn and how you can grow. You won't have all the answers in every moment, but you will always receive everything you need to take the next step through your discomfort with clarity and alignment. Everything comes exactly when it needs to.

EXERCISE YOUR
TRANSFORMATION STORY

1. Find your transformative moment.

Think back over your life and recall a particularly transformative period. It could be something in your college or university years, an experience starting or changing careers, or when you had a child. Maybe it's an important time you showed yourself the love you needed to receive or made a decision that showed a lot of belief in yourself. It could even be a new insight or perspective that changed how you saw yourself and your life. Trust the first thing that comes to mind and write a description of this transformation in your journal.

2. Activate your Line.

Do a Line Activation. As you sit in activation, try to remember the energy you were experiencing at this time by recalling some of the big emotions you were feeling and the things you did or thought in response to them.

3. Find the energetic pattern.

In the time leading up to and immediately following this transformative period, there will have been significant high and low vibrational experiences. These experiences will follow the pattern of energy (high, low, high, low, etc.), beginning with discomfort, and can help you see even the most familiar situation from the new perspective of soul growth and higher learning.

What was the moment of discomfort when your transformation began? This usually happens much earlier than the transformative moment itself. If you're not sure when your transformation began, activate your Line and ask your Highest Self for guidance. Trust what you receive.

In your journal, describe the major high and low vibrational experiences, starting with when your transformation began and then every significant one that followed.

How did this transformation alter your self-awareness, shift a perspective, habit, or belief, or alter your life path?

Optional: If you're having difficulty recalling a transformative experience in your life, use the following questions to help you understand how you respond to the low vibrational emotions where transformation begins. If you're closed off to your feelings, it can be harder to see how and when you're being supported to make changes in your life or learn more about yourself. Answer these questions with the goal of understanding if and how you're present in times when you're feeling a lot of energy or emotion.

Do you try to understand the reasons for your day-to-day emotions?

When you feel a lot of strong emotions, do you numb yourself to what you're feeling through distractions, blame, or ego-driven coping mechanisms?

In general, do you see events in your life as random or divinely guided?

When you're aware of your emotions and how you respond to them, you can see how your actions can make things feel bigger than they are, harder than they are, or more confusing than they are. Practice intentionally focusing your mind on each present moment, rather than reliving the experiences you've had or anticipating what's to come. This is your first step in spotting your patterns that are making it harder for you to learn from your emotions and see your experiences as opportunities for growth.

THE STORY OF MY TRANSFORMATION

Transformation can slowly unfold over several years in your life, so when you're in the middle of a transformative experience, you might not be aware of it. It may just feel like a difficult month or year. But when you zoom out and see things from above, you're able to make connections between the things you've done in the past that led you to the present and how you're being given opportunities for further growth ahead. Of course, it's much easier to do this in hindsight. For that reason, I want to share one of my transformation stories so I can illustrate what the major peaks of high and low energy can look like in a real-life scenario and how transformation requires us to see ourselves without judgment or shame, to confront our fears, and to trust the guidance we're always receiving.

The two most transformative moments in my life so far have been giving birth to my daughter and entering my Akashic Records for the first time. Leading up to both moments were times of deeply contrasting emotions, higher highs than I had ever felt and lower lows than I thought were possible, but every individual experience of them was an important step in my journey of learning how to accept the gifts I had been hiding from my whole life and to see my soul for the first time. I want you to see the incredibly deep and profound healing we can experience when we embark on the road back to who we've come here to be.

For the first thirty years of my life, I didn't see myself for who I am. Or, more accurately, I didn't allow myself to see. I hid from almost everything that makes me who I am, every unique gift my soul brought into this life. I was so afraid of my spiritual gifts that for many years I did everything I could to shut them down. I didn't want any part of them, and I didn't want anybody else to know what I could do, everything I could see, all of these things that kept happening to me. I wanted to be in the dark about all of this and, as a result, I was afraid of the dark.

Since I was a very young child, I struggled with sleep anxiety. The night was the scariest time for me. That's when I saw things, when I felt things, and when I heard things. The thought of these things happening would keep me awake every night, frozen in my bed, scared and anxious. I remember being in the second grade and every afternoon, sometime around 3:00 p.m., the fear would enter my mind that I wouldn't be able to fall asleep that night. It was like a loop quietly replaying in the back of my mind, over and over and over: Will I be able to sleep tonight? Will I be able to sleep tonight? Will I be able to sleep tonight? My mom slept in my bed with me a lot during this time and still would into my early adolescence. My fear became so strong that even as I grew and could understand my gifts more, I was still afraid to be alone at night.

By the time I was a teenager I had learned how to completely close myself off to my gifts. I didn't have any of the scary nighttime experiences I did as a young child, and for the first time I felt like I could enjoy the night. I would often stay out late with friends, lying on the grass and looking up at the stars. Without knowing it, I was receiving Universal Activations just by seeing the beauty of the night sky. I may have closed myself off to my gifts, but I was still drawn to something about them. It's like my gifts were a bright light. I couldn't look directly at them, I wasn't ready. I needed to learn more about myself before I could work through the low vibrational energy my fear was feeding. But here I was, unknowingly receiving the contrasting high vibrational energy, and it was showing me what was on the other side of my fear; the divine energetic presence I felt when watching the stars was a reflection of that same energy inside me.

My gifts started to come on stronger when I was in my twenties, and my fear of the night returned. I knew a lot of people who passed away during this time, including my grandma, and I would receive communication from many of them, sometimes in my waking state and regularly in my dreams. My soul was pulling me to learn more about myself and my gifts and to begin bringing my purpose to light, but I was still too afraid. I would quickly feel overwhelmed by the "supernaturalness" of it all. I didn't feel like I could talk to anyone about it either. I told my friends bits and pieces of my experiences, especially if I had dreams that involved them, but for the most part I kept everything to myself. I felt really different, and I didn't want to draw extra attention to that. So when it came to the night, and I really was all alone, I found new coping mechanisms.

It was around this time that I began smoking cannabis almost every night before I went to bed. Many people use this plant as a way to open up their energetic connection, but I used it to numb myself from mine. Before going to sleep I would say out loud, "I don't want to see anything, I don't want to experience anything. Go away, just let me be." For the most part this combination worked, and I was so grateful that I had tools to peacefully support me. However, I wasn't addressing the energetic root of my fears, so it was never long before I was in another wave of sleep anxiety.

After approximately five years of its support, I stopped smoking cannabis. It no longer felt good in my body. I had also been receiving messages in the form of "thoughts" (I didn't know what messages were at the time) that it didn't need to be a part of my life going forward. Once again, my soul was encouraging me to get to know myself, to understand myself, and to begin working with my gifts. Of course, it was only because this tool was so effective in helping me curb my fear that I felt strong enough to give it up.

Messages are always delivered at the right time, and two years later I got pregnant with my daughter. Pregnancy can be uncomfortable at times, and for me, even more so at night. My body was constantly changing shape, making every night a new challenge to find a comfortable position and fall asleep. But this wasn't the only reason it was hard to sleep. My dreams became so much more active, and my gifts were strengthening in a way they never had before.

One night, I had a dream that I gave birth to a baby girl. She had a head full of hair, wide, alert eyes, and an intense gaze. The moment I held her, she looked up at me and began to speak. She told me how old she was in her previous life when she passed away. She told me the year she died and showed me an image in my mind of how it happened. She then said she had been in a peaceful in-between place waiting for a family to join. She chose Ben and me to be her parents and said she couldn't wait to come Earth-side to be in our family. I woke up and immediately knew that I had met the soul of the child I was carrying.

Contrasting with these amazing realizations of my gifts was the return of my anxiety, which made me feel as energetically low as my gifts made me feel energetically high. I felt as though I was losing grip on my fear and entering the unknown. I had no idea how to handle my rapidly developing energetic abilities. Numbing myself to this side of me was no longer an option either, because I didn't smoke cannabis or drink alcohol anymore. And after I had my daughter, I entered the darkest nightmare of my life so far: postpartum anxiety and depression.

While I was healing, I spoke with a doctor who specializes in awareness, prevention, and treatment of mental health issues related to childbearing. She taught me that if you're going to experience postpartum depression or anxiety, it will attach itself to a preexisting issue (for me that was my fear of the night and not being able to sleep) and come in difficult and intense episodes to completely expose it and bring it to the surface. My postpartum anxiety and depression were the beginning of my awakening to and remembering of who I am at a soul level. Although it was the most painful, scary, and challenging experience I had ever had, everything I had been hiding from and trying to escape was illuminated so I could finally begin to heal. My healing journey began in the discomfort of the lowest vibrations of fear and hopelessness that I had felt in my life.

For my first seven months of motherhood, I was experiencing a dense contrast of energy. I felt a new level of love for my child that I had never experienced before and was for the first time starting to acknowledge that my energetic abilities could be a gift not a curse. But seeing the new sides of my gifts gave my anxiety new fears to feed. I would lie in bed sobbing, so afraid to close my eyes. It was like I couldn't let go. I didn't know what I would experience if I fell asleep. Who would come visit me? What messages from the other side would I receive? Eventually I felt I had completely forgotten what it was like to be asleep. It was like a foreign language I couldn't speak. But it wasn't sleep I didn't know, it was myself.

When I first became aware that what I was experiencing was postpartum anxiety and depression, I remember telling my mother-in-law that every night I couldn't wait for the morning because it was then that I could see clearly. At night, it felt like nothing made sense—not my gifts, my energy, or my fears. So I would often stay awake, waiting for the sun to rise, when it felt like I could see everything clearly again.

I wasn't aware of it at the time, but it was during the day that I could ignore my feelings. I had a new baby to take care of, and I could clean the house, run errands, cook, and exercise. But at night, when my baby was sleeping and everything was still and quiet, I had to sit with myself and everything I was feeling, high and low. It was just me and my energy, and I had to deal with it.

I knew I needed extra support to help me manage my anxiety, so I could more fully explore what I was being guided back to. I called medical helplines, I spoke with nurses, I even had crisis workers in our home early in the morning after a night I didn't think I would make it through. Time and time again I was told the same thing: "You're a new mother; this is normal. Once you adjust to this major life change, you'll feel better."

One night in bed, after yet another panic attack, I whispered to Ben, "I don't know how much longer I can hang on." I didn't think I would die, but I didn't know how I could keep living. I wanted to run away and never come back. I didn't know where to go, just somewhere that was far enough for me to escape myself. He took me to a new doctor the next day and for the first time someone believed me that my anxiety and depression was not something that would go away on its own. The doctor told me that what I was experiencing was unfortunately quite common but could be treated. When he wrote me a prescription, I was so grateful and relieved, and I felt like I had hope for the first time in months.

At first, I took a medication aimed at calming my anxiety so I could sleep. This worked for a few weeks until my anxiety grabbed hold of new fears to keep me from sleeping. I returned to the doctor and he wrote me a script for an additional medication that would help chemically rebalance my body. Shortly after taking this medication in combination with the first one, I noticed my anxiety subside. It wasn't gone but it was manageable, and I was now in a mental and emotional state where I could address the energetic root of it.

Eventually, I got to a point where I was excited by my gifts, not scared of them. For the first time in my life, I wasn't allowing my ego to keep me safe by repeating my old patterns of numbing myself to my gifts. I had outgrown that. Everything was now new. Motherhood was new. Healing anxiety was new. I had never tried to heal it or even understand it. I had only ever wanted it to go away.

Once I reached a point within my healing that I could explore my gifts even deeper, I discovered the Akashic Records. It was all in divine timing. I couldn't have arrived at that point without all the pain that came before. I felt as though I had come home to myself, that I had finally discovered how to receive information when I wanted to and needed to, and how to finally begin controlling the gifts I was born with. Slowly, as I continued to see myself, I feared the night less and less. I felt safe, calm, and secure going to bed because I understood how my energy worked and how to manage my gifts. I learned, and accepted, that I feel the collective energy deeply within me. I feel the energetic shifts and the collective reactions to them. Having been supported by the chemical rebalancing medication and the soul work of embracing myself and my gifts, I was able to go off my medication and feel aligned, strong, and healthy within myself, as myself.

Then to my surprise, toward the end of 2019, I started feeling a lot of fear at night again. I lay in my bed, short of breath and panicked. I was beginning to sense how much the world was about to change in just a few months. I saw people getting sick. I saw people dying. I sensed a lot of major changes quickly approaching, and it scared me a lot because I couldn't understand it.

Healing is not linear. Everything you experience, even the darkest moments that make you feel like you've taken ten steps back in your healing journey, have come up for a specific reason in your soul growth. At that time, I was in a place where I could embrace this discomfort without the fear of succumbing to the depths of anxiety. I didn't rush through these feelings or numb myself from them. I wanted to understand them. I decided to go back on medication to support my energy management during this energetically heightened time so I could feel calm at night and get a restful sleep, giving me the mental, emotional, and energetic clarity during the day to process my messages and integrate the learning.

At the time of writing this book, I'm at a point where I have the tools and abilities to manage my energy on my own. I have cultivated a sacred connection with the night and spend hours beneath the dancing Northern Lights in the winter and the magical twinkling light from the fireflies in the summer. I'm no longer scared of the night because I'm no longer scared of myself. This helps me peacefully move through the contrasting emotions I sometimes feel from my gifts with trust and surrender, knowing that every situation is for my spiritual growth and soul evolution and, in time, the energy I'm feeling will pass.

It's common to feel a lot of contrasting energy, especially fear, when you're awakening to your soul connection. It can be scary to allow yourself to be guided by your messages. You don't know what's to come or what you'll confront in yourself. Remember that whenever you're in the moments of low vibrational energy, you're also receiving messages that give you the next step to take in your journey. Through all the contrasting emotions and challenging experiences, you are uncovering layers within you. There is no hiding anymore. Your transformation begins in discomfort, but it guides you through the most beautiful learning, growth, and soul evolution. Every moment is an opportunity to see something new within yourself.

CHAPTER 8

THE MIDDLE SPACE

THERE IS A SPRING OF NEW ENERGY IN YOUR STEP. YOU
REALIZE THAT YOU ARE TRANSFORMING. YOU REALIZE
THAT YOU ARE CHANGING. LIKE A CATERPILLAR
CRAWLING INTO A COCOON AND THEN CRAWLING
OUT AS A BUTTERFLY, THIS IS WHAT'S HAPPENING TO
YOU, AND YOU FEEL THIS. AND ISN'T IT BEAUTIFUL?
AND ISN'T IT WONDERFUL TO TAKE A BREATH
OF FRESH AIR IN A DIFFERENT WAY, TO GULP IN
THAT OXYGEN AND FEEL IT COATING YOUR LUNGS
IN A BRAND NEW WAY? IT GIVES YOU A SENSE
OF LIFE THAT YOU HAVE NOT FELT BEFORE.

- THE PINNACLE

Your Line gives you more than messages. When you align with this frequency, you can feel relief from the intensity of energy in your body and find a calming perspective to help you see every experience and emotion for what it can teach you about yourself and your soul growth. This state is called your Middle Space. It's like a breath of fresh air when the heavy energy of a situation feels like it will never lift, or when it's difficult to find your next step. Sometimes all you need is a shift in your energy to see things differently—opportunities instead of challenges, beginnings instead of endings, or love instead of fear. Your Middle Space gives you this perspective.

You can think of your Middle Space as the midpoint between the high and low energetic frequencies you experience. While you don't want to escape your emotions, you want to understand them and learn from them. But energy can feel so intense sometimes that it's hard to momentarily step out of your emotions so you can recognize what you're feeling and know why your energy changed. In every situation, you have a choice: you can let your experience shift your energy or you can use your energy to shift your experience.

Activating your Line shifts your energy, and your Line brings you back to the love flowing through you. You are supported and your messages will give you the guidance you need on how to feel different and respond to any situation in alignment. When you're in a low vibration, you can use your Middle Space to find the high vibration of love, support, and perspective to learn what this energy can teach you. And when you're feeling a high vibration, you can use it to see what you learned in a low vibrational experience that helped you get there. Your Middle Space will help you make connections between how you're feeling and the larger opportunities for learning and growth you're being presented with. This changes how you experience energy, even the challenging emotions you encounter.

Your Middle Space also helps you bring love to any situation. Instead of judging someone else (or yourself), you can see the energetic reasons for their actions. You don't have to agree with what was said or done, but you can understand the energy they were responding to (even if they didn't realize this). This can stop you from reacting in your usual way and help you to find a different way to respond from the energy you want to feed within you.

It takes practice to surrender to the frequency of your Line and allow it to shift your energy. Focus on your emotional state before activating your Line and pay attention to any changes you feel in your body as you sit in activation. If you were anxious, you will feel calm. If you felt alone, you will feel supported. It's an energetic reset back to the home base frequency of the divine love flowing through your Line.

OBSERVE AND RELEASE

You have come into this life to feel a wide range of human emotions. You briefly wear these emotions when you feel them, but they are not you. You can allow them to leave just as easily as you invite them (or they invite themselves) in. Your Middle Space can help you observe your emotions in addition to feeling them, so you can learn what they're here to teach you and then release them.

Are you angry, jealous, anxious, listless? Acknowledge your emotions but understand that you don't have to be pulled down by them. You can feel any emotion without being controlled by it. Return to your Middle Space and see this emotion as energy, just like you.

Your soul wants to move but your ego wants you to stay still, even in uncomfortable emotions. Your ego will try to tell you that your emotions are beyond your control, that how you're feeling is someone else's fault or that you'll feel this way forever.

Your Middle Space is like stepping outside of yourself to get a wider view of what's happening. All energy moves in waves—big or small, high or low—and all energy passes. When you're in your Middle Space you can see the energy approaching, like you're watching a rainstorm roll in, and know it will pass, just like the clouds clearing after the rain. In the meantime, what is it here to teach you? How can you grow from this experience? Can you find the high vibrational contrast and move through this experience with more emotional balance?

When you allow yourself to be guided by your messages, you will encounter new situations and experience the new energy that comes along with that. It's often in these times that you'll feel overwhelmed by everything you're learning and feeling. Your Middle Space helps you see everything you're saying, doing, and thinking for its energetic effect on you and the people around you. How do your habits affect your emotions? How does your low self-worth make it harder to show yourself the love you need to process energy? How are you projecting your insecurities onto others? How is your ego trying to keep you from making positive changes in your life?

Your Middle Space shines a light on where you're not showing yourself the love that's flowing through you and helps you see the small changes you can make so you can feel different, believe in yourself, love yourself, and trust yourself. Healing begins by finding gratitude for the challenging moments in your life. It's in these times that you're receiving beautiful but difficult opportunities to learn more about yourself. Your growth deepens the love you have for yourself and the love you show up with in the world every single day.

There will be times when it's difficult to find this gratitude or to feel rebalanced in your Middle Space. The energy of a situation can make you think your Line Activations aren't working because you only feel a slight and brief shift in your energy, or maybe you don't feel anything at all. You may doubt your messages as quickly as they come, or perhaps you don't trust that they'll change how you feel. During these times, it's important to show yourself love, first and foremost, by doing anything that's heart activating for you. Your Line is always available to you, and the change you feel while sitting in activation is there to remind you that you can always shift your frequency, even if it only lasts a few seconds.

There are also many ways you can shift your energy without activating your Line. You can use your Activation Points by connecting to the Earth or looking at the stars, singing an uplifting song or chant, praying to God or the Universe, or by reciting the self-love mantra you received from the exercise in chapter 5. Do something you enjoy that will redirect your focus away from your present situation. When you feel more supported, aligned, or loved, you can return to how you felt and learn what your emotions were teaching you about yourself and what you need in order to be in alignment.

A Line Activation doesn't permanently affix your frequency to the energy of your Line because energy is always moving. As energetic beings, we move along with it. We're supposed to feel our emotions—all of them—but your Middle Space is another support tool you can use to see every experience as a learning opportunity designed to support your soul awareness and growth.

EXERCISE THE MIDDLE SPACE OF YOUR TRANSFORMATION

The Middle Space is something you need to experience for yourself to fully understand how you can use it in your daily life. In this exercise you're going to use the perspective your Middle Space provides to reflect on the transformative period in your life that you wrote about in the previous chapter.

Please note that in this exercise you will need to take full responsibility for your actions and acknowledge how they and the energy you held shaped your experiences. You don't need to shame yourself, feel guilty, or worry you'll be punished by God or the Universe for how you responded to your energy. Instead, love yourself for everything that has happened and accept it with gratitude because it is part of your journey that led you here. This is all for your learning and growth.

If you need help releasing judgment or accepting responsibility, open yourself up to new stories you tell about yourself. Judgment prevents you from stepping into growth, and accepting responsibility empowers you to learn. Be receptive to anything coming through from your Highest Self. Every message you receive is sent in love, even if it means admitting you could have moved through a situation with more peace and perspective.

1. Activate your Line.

Begin by doing a Line Activation and pay specific attention to the change in your energy as you sit in activation. You may experience this as a shift in your thoughts, a change of mood, or physical sensations in your body.

2. Use your Middle Space.

As you sit in activation, recall the significant moments of the transformative experience you wrote about in the previous chapter. Use your Middle Space to be lovingly honest with yourself as you reflect on how you handled your emotions during this time. Were you lost in the waves of high and low energy, or did you try to gain a larger perspective of what was happening? If you need help, ask your Highest Self, How did I manage my energy during this time?

3. Journal.

Now that you've used your Middle Space to see a different perspective, answer the following questions in your journal:

What does my Middle Space feel like to me?

Did I use it during the transformative period in my life, even if I didn't realize it?

What habits, patterns, or conditioned beliefs about myself prevented me from seeing things from my Middle Space?

In addition to a Line Activation, what are other ways I can shift my energy to find my Middle Space?

Optional: Many people in our community have said they can shift their frequency and find their Middle Space by doing simple things like deep breathing, going for a walk, or listening to a song they love. As I shared with you earlier in the book, reciting a mantra while looking at yourself in the mirror is incredibly powerful. If you feel this would be a helpful tool for you to have, ask your Highest Self in a Line Activation for a mantra you can use to quickly find your Middle Space. Write this mantra down and recite it every single day, at least once a day, to help you get familiar with the frequency of the Middle Space.

FROM YOUR MIDDLE SPACE, YOU CAN SEE A NEW PATH AHEAD

When I got pregnant with my daughter, I was working at a job in social media marketing. When I told my employer I was pregnant, I was given a choice: forfeit my year-long maternity leave after three months and return to work or take my full maternity benefit and have no job to return to. There are legal protections in place here in Canada to ensure that pregnant women have a job to return to after their twelve-month maternity leave. However, my employer told me that since my job was a contract position, they were under no obligations to keep it open for me after my leave was up. It didn't sound fair to me. I felt I was being discriminated against because of my pregnancy, but I also knew that contract positions, even those like mine that are renewed year after year with no formal discussions between the employer and employee, were ambiguous enough that they could make a legally legitimate case.

I was furious and I let this anger drag me down into a low vibrational space, where my fear and panic began to take over. Ben and I relied on my income as well as his to cover all our expenses, not to mention the soon-to-be added costs of raising a child. How were we going to afford everything?

I met him at a coffee shop an hour after my employer told me the news. "What are we going to do?" I asked him, through tears.

Had I managed my energy differently, I would have been more receptive to the messages I was receiving, which were telling me to trust that what was happening was for my growth. Instead, in my fixation on finding a loophole that would let me keep my job and take my maternity leave, we decided to get legal advice. I spoke to a couple of lawyers and for a few days considered taking my employer to court. Throughout all of this I was in a constant state of stress and anxiety, which under normal circumstances wasn't how I wanted to feel, but I was also pregnant and whatever I was feeling, my growing baby felt, too. It wasn't healthy for either of us.

After a week of deliberating, of replaying the situation in my head again and again, feeding the stress and anger and fear and allowing it to grow bigger and bigger, I received a message through my Line: "Release it. Let it go. This will all be okay." This was the contrast of everything I was feeling. My ego was a driving force in fighting for my job. It was trying to keep me safe by having things stay the same. But the high vibrational energy of trust, acceptance, and gratitude coming through my Line helped me see this experience as an opportunity to do things differently, to live differently.

I had always wanted to work for myself and here was a chance to do it. And even though I had no idea how I would bring money in, I felt supported by something bigger than me. I was ready to take this step. With a deep exhale and a sudden belief in myself and my messages, I signed off to keep my full maternity leave and effectively relinquish my job.

I had found my Middle Space, and it helped me see a new path unfolding in front of me. Although this didn't immediately change my situation and eliminate more low vibrational emotions or difficult experiences on this journey, it changed my perspective, and this was another step in trusting that my messages were guiding me down a new path back to myself.

It is a lifelong practice to find your Middle Space and, like all practices, you'll get better at it the more you work at it. As you begin to become familiar with the frequency of your Line, you shouldn't expect yourself to be in your Middle Space through every difficult energy you experience. There will be days, weeks, or months in your journey where you feel like you're out of alignment more than you're in alignment, and this is okay. Approach these moments with love for yourself and accept that there is always something for you to learn. Sometimes you need to act out of alignment to learn what you need to be in alignment. You may need to feel as though you are completely lost to rediscover yourself. When it feels like you're off course and you don't know who you are or where you're going, use your Middle Space to learn what the situation is teaching you about yourself and what your next step should be. This is how you walk down the path of growth and transformation.

CHAPTER 9

THE LIGHT OF
YOUR SOUL

THE DARK IS A PLACE OF KNOWING BECAUSE WHEN
THERE ARE NO DISTRACTIONS FROM BRIGHT LIGHTS
AND SUCH BRIGHT KNOWING, THE TRUTH IS THERE FOR
YOU, REVEALED AND SHOWING. THERE ARE ALWAYS
FLICKERS OF LIGHT WITHIN YOU, GUIDING YOU HOME,
BACK TO YOURSELF. DO NOT FEAR THE DARK.

- THE PINNACLE

You're learning more about your soul every day that you use your Line, every time you act on a message, find your Middle Space, or see the contrasting energy of a situation you're moving through. Over time, the connections you make between everything you've learned will reveal new ways your soul wants to express itself. These discoveries fill in the picture of your aligned self and help you see what your soul has brought into this life to help you live as this version of you. Your life isn't random. You are not an accident. You are here for a reason, and you've come into this life with unique gifts, purposes, and lessons to learn so you can infuse the beauty of your soul in everything you do. When you use one of your gifts, learn something from one of your soul lessons, or express your purpose, you will feel a spark of light inside you. Follow this light; it is your soul shining for everyone to see. It is guiding you home, back to yourself.

Your gifts, purpose, and lessons work together in this life to provide unparalleled insights into who you are. Your gifts light you up and light up the people around you. They are not designed to be kept to yourself. Your gifts bring you love, freedom, and joy, and when you share them with others, they also receive that love and joy. When you use them, you'll feel a deep sense of alignment and can learn how they help you express your purpose in this life.

Your purpose is your soul's full expression. It's how your soul wants to move through life. You will have many purposes throughout your life, because you are always learning, growing, and evolving, and every purpose will be rooted in divine love and collective healing.

Your most important purpose is to, simply and profoundly, experience this life. The Pinnacle have said that you are here in this physical body to feel emotions and learn from your experiences. This is how you grow and how your soul evolves. I share this with you because we often take this life for granted and forget that learning how to live as a human, how to understand the depths of our emotions and see the larger reason for every experience, is why we are here. Live with curiosity and be open to learning. As you learn, you grow. As you grow, you come into your soul expression.

You can't live out your purpose without using your gifts, and if you have any insecurities or fears around them, or if you don't think your gifts can help anyone, these feelings may be rooted in one of your lessons that are here for you to help you grow as a person and evolve your soul.

Your gifts, purpose, and lessons are woven together and there is no set order in which you'll discover them. This can make it seem confusing or overwhelming to begin thinking about them, but you can be certain that you have all of them. By opening your awareness to these parts of your soul, you will begin to learn a little more every day.

YOUR GIFTS LIGHT YOU UP AND SHINE BRIGHTLY INTO THE WORLD

Like a snowflake, you are perfectly unique, and so are your gifts. Even if you share the same gift with someone else, like a gift of communication, you express this gift in a way that nobody else can. When you use your gifts, you feel most like yourself. You feel aligned. Your soul brought your gifts into this life for you to share freely with the world. Your gifts bring you out into the world. When you use them, you are lighting yourself up at the same time as you light up everyone around you.

Your gifts don't have to be difficult to find within yourself, either. Most likely, you're already using one of your gifts, but because it's so familiar to you, you don't recognize it. For example, if you have a gift of finding beauty in everything, you can express it in so many ways, like by simply seeing the everyday harmonious beauty of the natural world that others don't notice, plating a meal with attention and care, rocking your personal fashion style, or designing websites. What unites these different expressions is the energy you feel when using your gift.

Your gifts shift your frequency into alignment with your Line and express a part of your soul that wants to shine. They provide a soul-level connection, and the love you're then aligning with will resonate deep within you and radiate to everyone around you. When you use your gifts, you're not only fulfilling a part of yourself, you're also supporting those around you. The light of your soul will reflect back to them the light they hold within. They will see your gifts and feel inspired to find their own, so they can shine just as brightly.

There are many people in our community, including Ben, whose gift is creative expression. For a lot of them, one of their gifts is related to a particular creative skill, like music, painting, photography, or writing. But creativity extends beyond the arts. You can be creative in the way you show love to your friends or in your approach to problem-solving. The energy you feel when expressing your gifts can also support you in discovering other areas in your life where you can use them or even in realizing other previously unrecognized gifts.

You have many gifts, and different ones will be activated at different times throughout your life because your gifts are meant to support you through specific stages of your journey. You may already have an idea of what some of your gifts are, or maybe you've never considered that your unique qualities are actually gifts from your soul. It's common for our community members to see their gifts for the first time during a transformative experience, like the ones discussed in chapter seven. It's in these times of massive learning and energetic contrast that you can see things about yourself that you thought were common as actually very special and unique to you. Your gifts can also help you feel the high vibrational contrast to a low vibrational experience you're moving through.

The one gift you don't need to question if you have is the gift of receiving messages through your Line. You were born with the ability to do this because you have a soul. Receiving messages is your birthright. You are always receiving messages even when you're not aware of them, and it's your messages that will lead you to discovering the gifts you hold.

There is contrast in everything, including your gifts. You can use your gifts to serve only yourself or to spread low vibrational energy. If you have a gift of communication, you can spread rumours, slander, or lies and because of your gift it will be easy to make others believe you. But if you do this, you won't feel that spark of light within you. You can also use your gifts in a way that helps other people but not yourself. If one of your gifts is holding space for others, you can overextend your commitments to friends, family, or coworkers, and feel energetically depleted because you're giving too much of yourself away. You won't feel that spark of light within you if the energetic balance is off. You can avoid situations like this by being aware of your intention for using your gifts. What energy are you feeling in those moments? Is it in alignment with your Highest Self?

Your gifts are meant to bring you out into the world, and it's when you're using your gifts that you learn more about them and how your soul wants to properly express them. If you're doing something that only lights *you* up, or you're only doing it for *someone else's* benefit, it either isn't a gift, the energetic exchange is unbalanced, or the gift is not fully realized and there's more learning to be done about how you can use it in this situation.

Just like your messages, your gifts will lead you into uncomfortable experiences, where you're confronted by your fears, doubts, or insecurities. These are opportunities to learn more about the soul lessons connected to your gifts, which I'll discuss after the following exercise.

EXERCISE LEARNING TO SEE YOUR GIFTS

This exercise will get you started on discovering your gifts by looking at the things you enjoy doing, understanding the energy you feel when doing it, and learning how you can share this with others. As you complete this exercise, open yourself up to seeing the things that seem second nature to you as potential gifts.

1. Activate your Line.

Do a Line Activation. As you sit in activation, feel the divine love flowing through you. Feel the love you have for yourself. You are special and there are things you can do in a way nobody else can. When you're ready, ask your Highest Self the following question: What skills or abilities come naturally to me?

2. Journal.

Answer the following prompts in your journal:

How do you feel when you use these skills or abilities?

How do you use these skills or abilities in your life right now?

In what ways can you use these skills and abilities for others and yourself?

Optional: If you feel like you didn't receive any messages in your Line Activation or were quick to doubt what came through, review the list of love you created in the exercise in chapter 5. Is there anything on this list that is something you're naturally skilled at? You can also ask your Highest Self for a self-love mantra to help you see yourself for the unique and gifted person you are. Recite this mantra while looking at yourself in the mirror. When you're ready, activate your Line again and repeat the question in step 1 of this exercise.

YOUR LESSONS OF GROWTH AND EVOLUTION

When you act on the messages guiding you toward new opportunities or different ways you can use your gifts, you will find yourself in situations where you feel the energetic growing pains of your soul's evolution, and sometimes this growth can be a little painful. These growing pains are called your lessons. Your soul brought them into this life for you to learn from in order to support your spiritual evolution, but also so you can see how everything that makes you unique, including your gifts, is connected to your soul's other lives and experiences. They are another way your soul expresses its multidimensional self. When you become aware of your lessons, you can use your

Line to learn what they're teaching you about yourself and how you can use the high vibrational energy of your messages to manage the low vibrational energy they bring up within you.

If you've ever felt like you're constantly failing at something, if recurring fears always come to mind, if the reasons for not trusting or loving yourself have always been the same, you may have already experienced one of your lessons. Throughout your life you'll be presented with many opportunities to learn from your lessons, and what you learn can enrich your understanding of why you have the fears you do, why you struggle to show yourself love, why you doubt your messages, why you don't believe in yourself, why you get jealous or are quick to anger or hold grudges. Life is full of contrasting experiences and so are your lessons: the low vibrations of these soul wounds vs. the high vibrational healing you can experience by learning from them.

Your lessons will show up in your life as familiar situations, dilemmas, or challenges (feeling emotionally or energetically shaken, reverting to harmful patterns and habits, etc.) when you're struggling to move through and being pulled out of alignment by low vibrational energy. The specific circumstances of your lessons will look different as you move through life, but the energy of the lessons will remain the same. As you begin to understand what your lessons are, you'll be able to recognize the opportunities to learn from them because you're more familiar with what that energy feels like to you. In those moments, you can ask yourself why the energy of that lesson came up at this time. What were you doing, thinking, and saying? Did something make you nervous, worried, or afraid? What are the connections between what's happening in your physical life and what you're feeling in your energetic body? These connections will help you understand what your lessons are teaching you about yourself.

It's very common for lessons to be felt as a specific fear. The Pinnacle have said that your fears have roots in one or many of your soul's other lives and are brought forward into this life for you to heal, as exemplified by Ben's cyst. If you know that one of your lessons relates to one of your fears, you can learn how to identify a challenging moment as an opportunity to learn more about this lesson, including what you can learn from how you've managed this fear in the past, connections you can make between this life and the energetic roots of your fear from your soul's other lives, and how your messages are guiding you to move through this moment in alignment.

Your messages will guide you through your experiences with your lessons, often with practical advice that you can act on immediately. However, acting on your messages doesn't take away the low vibrational energy. It provides the high vibrational contrast, showing you what's on the other side of this experience: growth, learning, and deeper connection to your soul and Highest Self. Even when you're aware of the reason for an experience, you can still feel uncomfortable or in energetic pain. Sometimes, your soul needs to feel this discomfort in order for it to learn and grow.

When the low vibrational energy feels intense and all-consuming, find your Middle Space to remind yourself that energy is always moving. Just as you shifted your frequency to align with the frequency of your Line, you can shift the energy of this situation as well. However, if you find it too challenging to act on your messages, or if the energy makes it too difficult to find your Middle Space to see this situation from above, the most important thing you can do is love yourself for being here and doing this work and for your intention to learn more about your lessons and all the beautiful but challenging things that make you the unique soul that you are. You are love; it's running through you.

Imagine you are driving a car in the rain. The road represents your Line, and the raindrops are your lessons. When the rain begins to fall, it becomes harder for you to see the road. You can either focus on the rain covering the windshield or look past the droplets to focus on the road. When working through your lessons it's important to keep your focus on your Line because this is where you're receiving guidance on how to move through these experiences with awareness and love. When you move through your lessons in alignment with your messages, it's like you develop spiritual windshield wipers. You have help clearing the rain, the low vibrational energy, and suddenly, you can navigate through even the strongest storms in alignment.

Your lessons aren't something you ever fully overcome and leave behind. They are not a test that you pass and progress from or fail and have to repeat. Soul work is a lifelong journey, and your lessons are with you throughout your entire life so you can learn as much as you can about how your soul wants to grow and evolve in this life. Your lessons are not punishment from God or the Universe for anything you did or did not do. They're not something you "called in." They are beautiful, and often challenging, opportunities to learn more about your soul-self. Equally, you're also not punished by God or the Universe for how much you learn or do not learn from your lessons.

When I've shared with our community that their lessons will always be with them, they have felt deeply disappointed and defeated. If you feel the same way, take comfort in knowing that you will understand the energy of your lessons better the more you experience them. This will make it easier to see each new experience from above, to understand the energetic significance of the timing of these opportunities, and to learn how to manage your emotional reactions to this energy and what this particular experience is teaching you about yourself and your soul. Each experience will look a little different, but you are always connected to your Highest Self and to the messages of love, support, and guidance to help you move through any situation.

EXERCISE THE LESSONS OF YOUR TRANSFORMATION

Return to the transformative moment you wrote about in the previous two chapters. You've already reflected on the energetic highs and lows of this time and used your Middle Space to see how you managed your energy as you moved through this experience. Now it's time to look at any recurring situations, i.e., familiar low vibrational energy you felt or behavioral patterns you exhibited during this experience, to learn more about your lessons. You may find it helpful to review your notes from the exercises in the previous two chapters before proceeding.

1. Activate your Line.

Do a Line Activation with the intention of receiving clarity on your lessons but without the expectation of knowing everything at once. As you sit in activation, feel the love you have for yourself and for the lessons your soul has come into this life to learn. Use your Middle Space to release any judgment, shame, or fear you have around learning your lessons. You are supported, you are loved.

2. Spot the patterns.

Think back on the transformative period in your life you wrote about in chapters 7 and 8 and when you're ready, answer the following questions in your journal:

What was a recurring internal or external dilemma or challenge throughout this experience? Describe the circumstances of it (when, how, and with whom it came up) and how you responded.

Were you repeatedly confronted by the same fear, anxiety, or desire during this experience? If so, describe what it was and how you responded.

3. Find the lesson.

You most likely were presented with an opportunity to work through one of your lessons during your transformative period. Identifying your lessons is about trusting yourself and the knowledge you have in this very moment. There is no wrong answer when you're learning about yourself. Every insight you have is another step toward more awareness. When you're ready, answer the following questions in your journal:

Looking at the patterns of energy, recurring feelings, or familiar challenges in your transformation, identify one lesson that showed up for you during that time.

How did you respond to this lesson at the time?

What new information does this lesson give you about yourself and your soul journey?

YOUR PURPOSE IS YOUR SOUL'S FULL EXPRESSION

Your purpose beautifully draws on everything your soul has experienced and brought into this life for your growth and evolution, providing you with a unique way of shining as yourself in every decision, opportunity, and experience you move through. Together with your gifts and lessons, your purpose gives you a multidimensional soul context for everything about you. At its core, your purpose is an energetic expression, and when you are living out your purpose, you'll feel this energy in your body. It will light you up, fulfill you, and make you feel full of life and completely yourself. However, just like gifts, when you align with your purpose, you will be presented with opportunities to learn from the challenging energy of your lessons. Alignment is not a guarantee of an exclusively high vibrational life. It's an invitation to grow, and growth is not always comfortable.

Your purpose is general enough to be carried out in many different ways throughout your life but specific enough to you and your soul journey that only you can express it. This can make your purpose seem overly vague, but this is only because your purpose isn't just something you do; it is an aligned intention that you can carry with you every day. You can feel the energy of your purpose in the many different ways you live it out. Your soul doesn't want to be limited in expressing its purpose in just one area of your life. It wants this beauty to infuse everything you do.

Our community members have said that expressing their purpose makes them feel full of passion or gives them an extra spark of life within their heart. How you experience this energy may be different for you but know that your purpose will make you feel like you are being fully and truly yourself. There will be times when you find it easy to express your purpose and other times when it's very difficult and you want to shy away from it.

Your purpose is for your soul's evolution and for the benefit of the collective. When you are showing up in your purpose, you're full of love for yourself and others. It's something you do for yourself to fulfill your soul's desires, not to prove something to yourself or others. Your purpose helps you feel like your true self. It lights you up and lights up those around you because you're emanating the divine love flowing through you.

Many of our community members have tended to conflate purpose with career. This is understandable because many of us live lives that are structured around the working day. When we're children we're asked what we want to be when we grow up, and once we're adults, our jobs are where we spend most of our time, so it would make sense that our purpose would relate to a specific career. But your purpose is much bigger than any one job.

There are many members of our community whose purpose is to teach, but this doesn't mean that every one of them should be a schoolteacher.

Think about every moment in your day when you have the opportunity to be a teacher, to anyone including yourself, and the many different ways you can teach something. You don't have to stand at the front of a classroom. You can be a teacher to your colleagues in the workplace, your kids at home, your neighbor, or an online community. There are so many opportunities in a single day to live out this purpose, and the specific instances in which you can live this out will change from day to day.

As you move through life, the ways you express this purpose will shift as well. You will find yourself in new situations and around different people, and you'll want to express your purpose differently. Or you'll receive messages guiding you to a new understanding of your purpose and how you can live it out. The way I've expressed my purpose of making the Akashic Records more accessible has changed over the years. I started by offering client readings and talking about the Records on my podcast and social media. I then began teaching people how to read the Records. When I discovered the Line, I freely shared the Line Activation and developed courses to help people use their Line to access the wisdom of their Akashic Records. And then I wrote this book.

Finding your purpose is deep soul work, and I encourage you to be patient and not rush to premature conclusions. Your messages will guide you there, piece by piece, step by step, and when you make the connections between everything you've learned about yourself, you gain a deeper understanding of the reason your soul chose this life. Your gifts will support your purpose, and your lessons will help you express it with more confidence and love. It doesn't matter whether you're young or old or how long it takes to find it; you never arrive at an understanding of your purpose too late in life. Every piece of soul knowledge comes to you in divine time.

You may or may not have an idea of what your purpose is. Regardless of the level of awareness you hold, it's helpful to focus on your energy rather than trying to spot your purpose among the things you're currently doing. It's the *feeling* you have that's most important because this feeling is what shifts your frequency and what others feel from you. Your purpose may be quite general (like using your voice, lifting others up, being a leader, etc.) or specific (like my purpose of making the Akashic Records more accessible). Your purpose may also change throughout the different stages of your life.

Within every person's purpose are countless forms of expression and many different ways your gifts can help you. The thread connecting them all is the energy you feel while living it out.

Be open and receptive to the guidance you're receiving about your purpose and identifying a purpose that is different from what you thought previously. When you believe you've discovered a purpose for this stage in your life, you can learn how your gifts help you express it. The lessons you are learning from can give you the deeper energetics and soul context of your purpose. And your Middle Space will help you see from above so you can understand how your purpose gives you a specific intention for every situation.

Discovering your purpose can give you a false sense of completion, like you've learned the most important thing you need to do and that your work is done. But your purpose is one of many important and beautiful parts of you, and your learning is never complete. Your purpose will enrich the use of your gifts and the understanding of your lessons. When you are living out your purpose, you will be guided to opportunities for further growth, with all the accompanying challenges, energetic contrasts, and deep learning. Your purpose is your soul's full expression, but your soul is energy and energy is always moving. Your soul will continually grow and evolve, and your messages will guide you in every stage of this journey.

CHAPTER 10

MULTIDIMENSIONAL MESSAGES AND SOUL CONNECTIONS

JUST AS THE WINDS CHANGE, THE SEASONS CHANGE
AS WELL. ALLOW PEOPLE TO DRIFT, RELEASING,
ALLOWING. DO NOT HOLD SO TIGHTLY TO ANYONE
OR ANYTHING; IT IS ALL FLOWING AND MOVING,
EVERYTHING. BREATHE IN, BREATHE OUT, ALLOW IT TO
FLOW. IT'S WITHIN THIS SPACE THAT YOU WILL GROW.

- THE PINNACLE

Every message you receive is drawing from experiences in your soul's other lives that are relevant to your present situation. I call these multidimensional messages. You feel the energy of these messages, emotionally or physically, because your soul is speaking to you, and it sparks within you a remembering. You don't have to know the soul experience your message is drawing from to feel this remembering or to learn how the message applies to your life.

As you develop your soul awareness by learning about your gifts, purposes, and lessons, you'll start making connections between your messages and your soul, like how the life path you're being guided down supports you in learning more about your soul's lessons, what energetic roots your fears have in your soul's other experiences, or how your healing in this life spans time lines to heal soul wounds from your other lives.

Your messages will also guide you to people in this life with whom you have a soul connection. You may be in each other's lives for a specific purpose, such as to help you learn a soul lesson, or to share divine love with each other.

There are some messages that will transport your energy to specific experiences in your soul's multidimensional existence. You may feel like you've already had the conversation you're having or that you've previously been to the "new" city you're visiting. These feelings are commonly called déjà vu, and the feeling of already having lived through or having a memory of the present moment is a remembering of something from one of your soul's other lives.

There are multidimensional messages that feel like you're bending time and space and existing in two places at once—here on Earth and wherever it is your energy is visiting. These are commonly experienced with your soul's other lives on Earth. But you can also receive messages where you're energetically taken to places outside of this world so you can communicate with the energy of your guides, the energy of a deceased friend or family member, someone else's Highest Self, the Pinnacle, or any other energetic being that is coming through to support you. These require a deeper sense of soul awareness and connection to your Line.

When I first started teaching our Line Within community about multidimensionality, the Pinnacle gave me a variety of visuals and examples to illustrate this concept. Here's one way to think of it: Your energy is like the planet Saturn, and the rings surrounding your energy are the many other dimensions your soul exists within. In some of these dimensions your soul is living a physical life, which may be happening in your linear past or future. These lives may be lived on Earth, on other planets, or in other Universes. These experiences are continually orbiting around your energy, and in this way are all happening at the same time, regardless of whether, from the standpoint of this life, they're in your past or future. And because these lives are orbiting around you, your soul is continually receiving inspiration and information from them and sending them to you as messages through your Line.

You're receiving these multidimensional messages for a reason and in divine timing, even if they don't immediately make sense. I like to think of these, and all kinds of messages, as puzzle pieces. You may not have a connecting piece right away, but you know it will fit with something. In the meantime, writing down your messages, experiences, and anything else that feels connected and important (don't write off anything—there's energetic meaning behind every single experience you have) will help when you receive a message in the future that connects to something you've already received.

Line Activations will support you in understanding these experiences and making connections. However, it's important to remember that you're receiving everything you need to know in that moment to help you take your next step. So even if you want to know more right now, you may not learn anything else in your Line Activations, and as a result you may feel in the dark longer than you like. It can take time to decipher the meaning of these messages and learn what they're telling you about your soul. Multidimensional messages are beautiful moments of connection that span time and the cosmos, and they are here to help you know yourself and move in alignment with your Highest Self. You may want to know everything right away, but you don't need to. All you need to do is trust and move forward with what you're receiving.

MULTIDIMENSIONAL HEALING

Our community has received some truly beautiful and healing multidimensional messages. Parents have discovered connections with their children in their souls' other lives, and the information they received gave them new insight into their relationship dynamics. One mother had felt an unexplainably strong connection to her daughter from the moment she was born. It was bigger than the bond between a parent and child. She felt like she had already known her daughter for a lifetime. She learned that she and her daughter are sisters in another life, and what she was feeling was an energetic resonance in this life to an experience her soul is having elsewhere.

Other parents have discovered the energetic reasons for why disagreements with their children often lead to fights and the soul lessons their child or children are here to teach them. This information can help the parent break out of their emotional reactions or ego-driven habits that are keeping them from acting in alignment, from a place of love and understanding for themselves and their children. The lessons they learn can heal harmful patterns and support them in acting in alignment in their other relationships as well.

Another community member healed her persistent migraines through her multidimensional messages. Her grandfather had tragically taken his own life before she was born, and the pain she often felt in her head was like an energetic resonance of the trauma he inflicted upon himself. She communicated with her grandfather's energy and learned that this physical pain was an energetic remembering from her own soul. It turns out that one of her soul's other lives was as her own grandfather. In many cases we have other lives as our ancestors. In her present life, she was living with the trauma from the gun shot in her own energy field to support her in understanding the energetic root of her physical pain. Since making this connection and releasing the energy of the wound, her migraines have stopped and have not come back.

When you experience these soul remembrances or receive multidimensional messages, you're not physically traveling in time or space. But your soul isn't bound by the same restrictions your physical body is, and it's because of your energy that these experiences are possible. Sometimes your multidimensional messages will feel like any other message except that they are giving you information about another soul experience or perhaps many experiences that connect to your current physical life.

Other times you'll have a feeling or "memory" of another life come through your Line or you'll have a dream where you visit another world or you'll feel you've already experienced something that's happening in the present moment (a conversation, a thought, something you see or energetically receive). You can also feel this energy in your physical body, like it's saying to you, "Yes, this is true! Pay attention!" It can be incredibly subtle, a whisper-like knowing of truth and connection. Or it can feel like a rush of warm comfort, excitement, shivers, or goose bumps, sometimes even causing you to break out in a sweat, all while feeling the reassuring love from your Line.

SOUL JOURNEYING IN YOUR DREAMS

Something amazing happens when you go to sleep: your human ego steps aside and allows you to fully receive what your soul is experiencing. Your dreams are soul communication. They are full of meaning and can provide incredible context for your purpose, gifts, or lessons. When you're asleep you're more receptive to important information coming through your Line because your conscious mind is resting, and you're in a state of release and surrender. The ego-driven urges you may have to doubt your multidimensional messages melt away, and you're able to open yourself up to a vast array of otherworldly experiences.

You can travel to the other lives your soul is having, and visit other planets, galaxies, and energetic realms. Just like the Highest Realm I discussed in chapter 1, there are many other energetic realms you can interact with. The things we see and hear in our dreams aren't coincidences or a random and meaningless patchwork of subconscious thoughts and desires. Many of my Akashic Records clients would ask about the recurring dreams they had for most of their life and when we went into their Records, we learned that these weren't dreams they were having; they were experiences their soul was having in other lives.

I frequently visit a planet with beautiful rocky, red mountains and three moons in the sky. The sun is so large that it fills the entire sky as it sets. It's incredibly beautiful and my memories of this place are so vivid, it's as if I experienced them in this physical life. I wake up feeling like I just visited another home.

Your dreams can also give you a sense of closure for and energetic understanding of the relationships you've had in this life. Ben once had a dream where he was in an unfamiliar restaurant, walking between crowded tables and not knowing where to go until someone grabbed his arm. It was one of his former romantic partners whom he hadn't seen in ten years. They were in each other's lives for a brief and emotionally intense period and since then he had been trying to understand the reason for their time together. He knew they shared a soul connection but wasn't aware of the purpose for it.

In the dream, they greeted each other, and he put out his arms to hug her, unsure if she would accept. She did and as they embraced, he felt a warm sensation in his chest, like the divine love running through his Line was being activated. It was so strong that in that moment his awareness shifted. He knew he wasn't in the physical realm on Earth. His energy was somewhere else at the same time as his body was lying in bed at home. This experience opened him up to seeing the purpose for their connection: to share love with each other at a time in their lives when they each needed to receive it.

One of my most profound dreams recurred for years. In this dream, I am outside with friends under a bright sun. I walk down a street and enter a home with pale yellow walls. In one of the rooms there is a bed under a window. I sit on the bed, pull back the sheer curtains, and look out at a bright sky. The time on the clock next to the bed reads 3:00 a.m. I had so many visions of this home that for many years I couldn't remember if it was a dream or a memory from this life. But then I would remind myself that it couldn't be a memory. The sun isn't out at 3:00 a.m.; the sky is dark. In every dream it was always the same house, the same bed, the same window, and the same sun.

One night, over fifteen years after first having this dream, I came across a video of something called the "midnight sun." In certain areas in the Arctic Circle, such as Northern Canada, Northern Scandinavia and Europe, and parts of Alaska and Greenland, the sun never fully sets during the summer months. As soon as I saw the video, my entire body broke out in goose bumps, and my eyes filled with tears. I had found the sun from my dream! Suddenly, I began receiving messages through my Line that in this dream my energy was traveling to lives my soul is having in Lofoten, Norway, where in the summer months the sun is bright in the sky all night long.

The messages you receive in your dreams or in other multidimensional messages won't always make sense on their own. You will need to connect these to other messages coming through your Line and anything else you've learned about your soul journey to understand their full meaning.

Think of your multidimensional messages as stars. On their own, they are sparkly dots in the sky, but when you connect the dots, they form a constellation rich with meaning, insight, and wayfinding. Your multidimensional messages are memories separated by dimensions or lifetimes, but you can make connections between them to see the picture and understand the reason you're experiencing them.

SOUL CONNECTIONS

Throughout this book, I've encouraged you to use your Line to focus on *your-self*, learn about who *you* are, and receive the messages guiding *you* in *your* soul journey. You may have turned off the energetic faucet for some people in your life or established energetic boundaries with family or friends to help keep the focus on yourself. Living in your Line brings you back to your soul-self, but it doesn't mean that in this journey you're all by yourself.

I've learned from the Pinnacle that every relationship you've ever had, currently have, and will have is planned by your soul before you were born into this life and designed for a specific purpose. On our own, we don't learn as much as we do with each other. We need our connections with others to help us grow. We mirror our gifts and talents to one another. We trigger one another and shine light on our lessons and egos. We help each other keep moving along our aligned paths.

The soul connections you have with people can take different forms and some will feel more significant than others. In some cases, two souls arrange a brief encounter in this life for mutual growth and evolution. In other cases, two souls are energetically and eternally bound and can come in and out each other's lives in many different lifetimes to support, teach, love, and share guidance. Your soul connections will show up in your life whether you're aware of this special bond or not. They can be people in your life right now, people from your past, or someone you'll meet in the future.

There are two types of connections that are important to discuss here because the relationship you have with them will look different from other relationships in your life. These two connections are soul contracts and soul family. These people are in your life for a specific reason, and when you're aware of what you're here to learn from each other, you will rapidly deepen your soul awareness and access a new level of healing and growth.

SOUL CONTRACTS

Soul contracts are agreements made between two souls (at a minimum) to meet at a specific time in a physical life for a special purpose. This purpose can be a lesson both souls want to learn and grow from, an opportunity to heal something within the souls (a shared trauma or fear from another life, for example), or to create something to share with the world. The agreement creates a special energy that brings the souls into each other's physical lives and supports the fulfillment of the contract. A soul contract can be short-term or last a lifetime. For example, the contract we hold with our children lasts a lifetime, but a soul contract with a friend, coworker, spouse, or partner can have a more limited term. While you have a soul connection to everyone in your life, you don't have a soul contract with all of them.

The people you have soul contracts with will show up in your life whether you're aware that you share this connection or not. What needs to happen for the contract to be fulfilled will happen, even if neither person knows of the shared soul connection or learns what was meant to be learned. When the contract ends, the energetics between the two people will change. This can be felt as tension, friction, distance, or a sense of not being on the same page anymore. It can feel like you're seeing a different side of a person or that you or they suddenly changed.

At this point, the two people can either peacefully part ways or choose to redefine their relationship based on the new energetic dynamic between them. When the energy changes, the patterns between the two people will need to change as well. This takes time and patience and usually involves both people coming back to themselves and their Line and doing inner healing before building a foundation of new energetic patterns and routines for the relationship going forward. This can be an emotionally strenuous experience but, as always, your messages will guide you and the energy of your Line will reflect divine love to you.

In the spring of 2020, as most of the world was entering its first pandemic lockdown, I experienced a beautiful soul contract. I had seen this person often for many years and had never felt anything other than friendly energy. But in one interaction, on one afternoon, I felt the energy between us shift. This person is also an entrepreneur like myself, but unlike me, his business was about to change significantly. I remember being overwhelmed with sadness for him and felt responsible for making sure he and his business were okay. I visited the business every single day to financially support him, bring friendly, loving energy, and heard about the creative new ways his shop was adapting and persevering.

At the time, my family and I were preparing to buy a house. I was aware of how privileged we were to be in such a fortunate position when so many others were experiencing such incredible loss and uncertainty. Although I was excited about this opportunity, I was also uncomfortable talking about it. One day, I told him about a house we had looked at and that we were considering putting an offer in for it. He became so excited for me, animated with an energy he hadn't shown me before, and encouraged me to buy the house. Energetically, everything felt far beyond the present, physical life. The emotional reaction I had to his words of support felt like more than friendship but it wasn't romantic either. It was bigger than that.

I could sense a deep connection between us and so I decided to enter my Akashic Records to research more. I learned that in one of my soul's other lives in the 1940s we were married and living in Odessa in the Ukraine. We were enjoying a beautiful life together when the Second World War broke out. I saw how our lives, like many others, were tragically uprooted and the struggle we endured in the tumultuous period that followed. I also saw how his life ended. I then learned that in this life our souls arranged a brief contract during a time of uncertainty and instability to remind each other of our resilience and to continue moving forward with faith and strength.

I made these connections in my Akashic Records, but it wasn't until after I closed the Records and received a message from my late grandma through my Line that I was brought to tears. Moments before my grandma transitioned from her physical body and back into the energetic realm, she called out, "Odessa! Odessa! Take me, Odessa!" I thought she was calling out to an angel or a light being for comfort, but after I learned about this other soul life, I received through my Line a beautiful, time-bending, multidimensional message that she was also giving me a clue about Odessa that would only make sense years after she said it. When I made this connection, her voice came through to me: "Ashley, you need to teach the world about soul contracts, soul family, and soul relationships." Within the next few days, I realized that this friend and I had both fulfilled our ends of the contract; it was complete, and the energy shifted back to how it always had been.

SOUL FAMILY

Your soul family are the souls that are from the same star energy as you. The energetic bond you share with your soul family is deeper than anything a human emotion can create. When you meet in this physical life, you are here to share soul love with each other. This love is far beyond human love. It's a nonjudgmental, all-forgiving, peaceful and whole. This love is woven through the souls, eternally bonding them together across time and space. As a soul family, you use this love to catalyze change and growth in each other's lives, helping each other become a more fully realized version of your soul-self.

You have many soul family members, and in this life, you will meet or have already met some of them. But there are many others who you may never meet. The encounters you share with your soul family are sacred. You'll feel a unique and immediately deep connection with them. I have said that your messages can sometimes feel like a remembering of something you knew deep within. Your soul family sparks a similar but infinitely deeper remembering because you are feeling an energetic connection that spans lifetimes and dimensions of existence.

Different soul family members will come in and out of your life to match certain chapters of your life. At any one time, you will only be working with a few of them. The work you do with soul family members is different from your soul contracts. Your soul family is here to help you make changes in your life and support you in deep learning and understanding your soul purpose. They may reflect your gifts to you and support you in sharing them with the world, or they may guide you to soul healing you're being called to do.

You may have close physical contact with your soul family, or you may be separated by an ocean and never physically meet. You can feel your energetic connection over the greatest distance, just like you can feel the divine love that comes from the Highest Realm running through you. The Pinnacle have said about soul family that "you're branches on the same tree. Even if you do not touch, you share the same roots."

When you often dream about the same person, even if you haven't had contact with them in a long time or perhaps have never had contact at all, you're most likely dreaming about a soul family member. I've learned from the Pinnacle that souls that repeatedly visit us in our dreams are souls that come from the same star energy as us.

A lot of people in our community have shared that they dream about a past lover, and in these dreams, they are seeing experiences that didn't happen in their current life. It's like they're seeing another life in some other dimension. They'll wake up thinking about this person, longing for a renewed connection with them or feeling a deep love for them despite being in a fulfilling, loving, and committed long-term relationship or marriage. They don't know if this means they're supposed to get back together with them or if it's a sign that they're not truly happy or fulfilled in their current relationship.

In a lot of these cases, they have discovered through their Line that the energy they are feeling is a deep energetic connection to a soul family member. The love they're feeling is the divine love they are meant to share with soul family, but because of their history they've confused it with romantic love. These types of realizations provide massive clarity on potentially confusing feelings and help release any shame or guilt for thinking about an ex while being in a committed relationship.

The underlying energy of soul contract and soul family experiences is love. Love for yourself and love for others. Love to help you understand and heal. Love is the most profound emotion we can hold with one another, and it spans the many dimensions our soul exists within. Any love felt between you and someone else in this life will live on in your soul, even if the interaction or relationship resulted in loss, heartache, pain, or fear.

In the energetic realm, your souls only know love. This love is the energy running through your Line; the same energy that is infused into every message you receive. This love unites souls for eternity and when you connect again with these souls through your multidimensional messages, you'll receive love to help you release fears, overcome doubts, learn from your lessons, discover how to use your gifts, or any other support you need to bring you back to yourself.

EXERCISE YOUR
MULTIDIMENSIONAL MESSAGES

In this exercise, you'll open yourself up to seeing the multidimensional messages or soul connections you've already experienced. Writing down these experiences will help validate their significance and keep them in your awareness.

1. Activate your Line.

Begin by activating your Line, and as you sit in activation, think of yourself as an energetic being, able to transcend the physical limitations of this world, move through time and space, and connect to other experiences your soul is having.

2. Journal.

When you're ready, use the following questions to uncover the multidimensional messages you've already received or the experiences or feelings you have had that you believe have their energetic roots in one of your soul's other experiences. Allow yourself to fluidly write everything that comes through, withholding analysis, judgment, shame, or doubt.

This is a longer exercise, and you don't need to finish it in one sitting. Write about the experiences in your awareness right now. If you don't have anything to write for a section right now, proceed to the next one. You can return to this exercise at any time.

DREAMS

Recall any dreams (recurring or stand-alone) you've had that you believe have a deeper meaning. These can be dreams about places, people, time periods, or experiences from another life or in another dimension. If you remember them now, take that as a sign that there's a deeper meaning in them for you.

Describe these dreams in your journal, writing as much as you can but only what you remember, and answer the following question after each one: What was going on in your life at the time you had this dream?

TIME

You can receive multidimensional messages as a feeling of connection to a specific time period. We can often mistake these as an interest in history when it's our soul sharing with us information about another life it is experiencing during this time.

What time periods do you feel connected to?

How does this time period (or periods) make you feel?

Describe any experiences you've had (dreams, remembering, inner knowing) of soul connections to these time periods.

PLACES

There can be places in the world that give you a sense of home even if you don't live there or have never traveled to them. This feeling could be your soul signaling you to a life it is having there.

What places have you felt drawn to but have never visited in this life?

Do you know what it is about these places that pulls you in?

Have you had an experience that first made you aware of this connection? Describe this experience and when it happened.

PEOPLE

You can have soul connections to people you've met in this life, whether it's a soul contract or a soul family member. They can come into your life to deliver a message, help you learn a lesson, or share divine love and support.

Are there people in your life, past or present, that you believe you have a soul connection to?

What is/was your relationship with them like?

What does this soul connection feel like to you?

Optional: Read through your notes when you've finished and then do another Line Activation. As you sit in activation, close your eyes and ask to see any of your soul's other lives that relate to something you wrote about. Trust anything that comes through, even if it's small or simply a confirmation that you've made a connection between something you experienced in this life and something your soul is experiencing in another. Write down what you receive in as much detail as it was delivered to you.

DOTS IN THE SKY

Your soul journey is like a constellation in the night sky. Each moment is a star, a dot in the sky. As you trace a line from one experience to another, which can be years, dimensions, or lifetimes apart, you will start to see a fuller picture, a glittering shape of understanding. This understanding may take years but every realization you make will come when you need it. You may make one connection now and realize what it means to you in this moment, and years later another meaning comes to you to support you with something you're moving through then. Trust the meanings that come to you in the moment and be receptive to how these meanings change as you receive more multidimensional messages and make more connections.

As you grow and transform you will bring new insight and meaning to your multidimensional messages. You will learn more about why you received them and how they are here to help you in this life. Your energy is always moving and changing, and the multidimensional messages you're experiencing will change along with you.

Your spiritual journey and your journey to come home to yourself isn't linear. You may have moments of amazing clarity only to feel like a student again the next day, trying to relearn what your soul needs to feel aligned in a new stage of your life. In every situation you are receiving everything you need to adapt and align. Surrender to the divine timing of your multidimensional messages and remember that you know everything you need to in this moment to take the next step back to yourself.

CHAPTER 11

A NEW
FREQUENCY FOR
A NEW WORLD

IN ORDER TO BECOME ALL THAT IT IS YOU DESIRE,
YOU MUST BE AN ACTIVE PARTICLE OF LIGHT
IN THE FULL ANATOMY OF THE COLLECTIVE
EXPERIENCE. AND IN ORDER TO BE AN ACTIVE
PARTICLE OF LIGHT, YOU MUST BE YOURSELF.

- THE PINNACLE

We are living in a new time. A time of miracles. A time of evolution in our energetic abilities. A time when coming back to ourselves shows us a new way of coming together as a collective. The world has received a new energetic frequency that is designed to awaken every one of us to a new level of soul awareness. This frequency fills you with love. Show it to yourself so you can receive your messages with full trust that they're guiding you to the life your soul came here to live.

Every time you act in alignment with this version of you, your energy spreads. It continues to move and move—it expands, it grows, and it reflects to others their own soul calling out to them. For the first time in human history, the energy is supporting you in being yourself because when you're living as your aligned self, you're serving others. This is the new frequency of the New World. It is time to return to yourself, to step into your glory and shine your light on yourself and everyone around you.

This new frequency came to us at the beginning of 2020, and every year since it has provided new opportunities to know ourselves and our soul. The Pinnacle said that soul awareness helps us love ourselves more deeply, and that this love is what will allow us to come together as a global community in a more harmonious way than we ever have before.

This energy arrived at a time of great energetic contrast within the collective. Throughout that year, there were four heightened waves of this energy, and the emotions these waves triggered within each of us were beautiful, if difficult, entryways into who we are in our soul. You didn't have to know about this new frequency or have made the soul connections at that time to have felt these waves for yourself. Around the world, people were awakened to buried trauma and emotional healing within themselves and the collective. They worked together, organized, rallied, spoke up, spoke out, and energetically linked hands in a new way. We embarked upon a new journey of healing.

When an energetic frequency is received within the physical realm, there is and always will be contrast. And when there's contrast, there is learning, growth, and evolution. The Pinnacle have said that in the New World, "the colors are brighter and the sorrows are heavier." Emotions of love, connection, awareness, and acceptance were contrasted by intense fear, anger, and division. During these waves, these contrasting energies swept across the planet quicker than energy had ever spread before.

This was also a time when many of us were isolated from each other, alone in our homes and alone with ourselves, maybe for the first time in a long time. The Pinnacle said in that year that you can no longer hide from yourself. "Now is the time to know yourself," they told me. People changed their daily routines, quit jobs, ended relationships, explored hidden talents, and tried new things. So many people acted on their messages without even knowing they were responding to their soul. Everyone acknowledged that this energy (or "time," if they didn't talk about energy) was different. Things had changed. There was an opportunity to transform ourselves and our world.

This new frequency has opened our hearts, activated a deeper love within us, and brought us into a closer connection with ourselves, our communities, and the Earth. This frequency is supporting you right now in whatever you're moving through in this stage of your soul journey.

We are living in the New World, where healing ourselves helps heal others and the planet. It begins by coming back to yourself and your messages. This is spirituality for the New World. Being yourself is a spiritual practice.

SPIRITUALITY IS SELF-AWARENESS

There have been many times throughout human history when global low vibrational energy was met with the high vibrational contrast of collective spiritual awakenings. In 1945, when the first atomic bomb was being dropped in Hiroshima, Paramahansa Yogananda was writing *Autobiography of Yogi*, a book that would inspire spiritual awakenings in millions of readers for years to come. Then in the 1960s, the time of the Vietnam War and the "hippie" counterculture, humanity experienced a new frequency of love, consciousness, and spiritual connection. We are living through another one of those times right now. What's different this time is that we're not waiting for a leader to show us the way forward. We're being awakened to ourselves.

In the past, people looked to a prophet, priest, or political leader to tell them what it means to be a spiritual person and how to live a pious life. But the energy of this time no longer supports that approach. The collective spiritual energy is breaking down and diffusing to support you in being your own spiritual guide so that together we can all create a world where we can learn from each other but lead ourselves.

There are thousands of spiritual leaders today sharing their teachings in books, podcasts, online courses, and social media accounts, yet there isn't one person that is shifting the paradigm on their own. It is the result of a collective effort, each person using their gifts, acting on their messages, telling their stories, and inspiring others to do the same. You can benefit from the energy of the teachers in your life, whether you have a personal relationship or follow them online, but nobody can tell you the specific soul work you've signed up for in this life. Only you can do this work.

But this doesn't mean you are alone. You always have your Line connecting you to the wisdom of your soul, and you have your cosmic team, energetic guides, God or Source, the Universe, and a wealth of energetic support surrounding you. This new frequency liberates and empowers you to be your own guide and discover who you are, why you are here, and what you can bring to the world. Self-awareness is the new spirituality.

The New World we're living in has been associated with many transitional points, and there are two I want to briefly discuss: the astrological Age of Aquarius and the Second Coming of Christ.

The Aquarian Age is said to bring massive transformation in technology, evolutionary advancements of our species, and a great coming together of humanity. On December 21, 2020, the day of the solstice that year, when the energy of the fourth energetic wave of the New World frequency was peaking, Saturn and Jupiter moved into alignment in the astrological sign of Aquarius, which is associated with revolutionary thinking, innovation, and social progress.

This alignment, or "conjunction," was called the great conjunction because at their closest distance, the two planets were only a tenth of a degree apart. While Saturn and Jupiter align around every twenty years, they hadn't been this close to each other since 1623, almost four hundred years earlier. When these two planets are conjunct, they are so close to each that they look like one giant star when viewed from Earth. This conjunction is sometimes called the "Christmas Star" because some believe that the Star of Bethlehem that led the three wise men to Jesus's manger wasn't a single star but this same great conjunction.

Like all Earth and Universal Activations, the timing of this conjunction wasn't a coincidence. I believe it signaled a major shift in the energy of the time, a high vibrational contrast to the low vibrational energy around the world at the time.

People have often associated the Age of Aquarius, or this millennium, with the return of Christ on Earth. Interestingly, when this new frequency started to illuminate our planet, I began channeling the energy of Jesus in my personal Akashic Records, as well as in many of my client's Records. This energy felt so different than the Jesus I heard about in church as a child. This Jesus was a spiritual guide, not a religious figure; an energetic being of unconditional love, and, to me, a breath of fresh air. In my Records, he explained to me that he is Pleiadian energy and that his "return" in this era isn't a physical return. It is a return of his divine love energy, the highest vibration of the New World frequency. This is the love we have flowing through our Line. By receiving this love for ourselves and sharing it with others, we're supporting the growth of this new love frequency and the healing of our planet.

A lot of our community members come to this work with significant religious trauma. The wounds of institutionalized religion can be so deeply embedded within many of us that reading the name Jesus or talking about the Divine can trigger painful memories of things done in the name of God. This new frequency is helping us heal centuries of religious guilt, shame, abuse, and fear. It supports us in separating the dogma of religion and the energy from which it all began.

God is a name we've given to an energy we all feel. The Universal One energy, Source Energy, the energy we come from. And you are simply, truly, and magnificently an expression of this divine energy. God lives within you, and so the moment you meet yourself, you meet God. Since you are always and forever changing, you must continue knowing yourself and understanding the love running through you. It will always guide you to yourself, to your divine essence, no matter how much you change. The Pinnacle said, "Connect back to the energetic essence of you and just be. This is spirituality."

The Line isn't a religion. The Pleiades aren't the church. The Pinnacle aren't the priests. Every message you receive is coming from something your soul is experiencing here or in another life. This knowledge comes to you because it is you. The Line is your constant in a world with so many influencing ideas, opinions, and energetic pressure of who you should be and how you should act. The messages you receive will sharpen your discernment so you can understand what an aligned expression of your soul looks like to you.

You were born into a family with a history and a culture, you were assigned a name and a gender, and you were taught specific values and maybe raised to practice a certain religion. These things may fit you or not. Finding your way back to yourself means going through everything handed down to you and every identity trait you adopted, so you can learn what supports you in living in alignment with your Highest Self. As the Pinnacle said, "You were never supposed to be the way you began; your roots are just one part that hold you together and allow you to expand."

THE WORLD IS A MIRROR

In every moment, you're in control of what energy you're holding within and what energy you're emanating out into the world. As I discussed in chapter 6, we are sponges absorbing the frequencies of an energetically dense world, and sometimes we're not aware of how the energy we're holding is affected by everything we encounter in our day. Just as you can be unaware of the connection between how you feel and the energy you let in, the frequencies you project out into the world shape your experience of this physical reality.

Your energy will change the things that you notice and the meaning you attach to them, the connections you make, the judgments you hold, and your willingness to understand how everything you see is telling you something about yourself. The world is a mirror, and what you see reflects something within you: a trigger, a lesson, a soul connection, an emotional trauma, a message.

As always, your ego will try to stop you from taking ownership of your energy. It will try to minimize your power, place the blame for your feelings on someone or something else, reduce the divine glory within you so you stay the same and do nothing. When everything is someone else's fault, the ego can remain still. This is what it wants. But your messages want motion. They want you to move, dance, and play.

To help overcome your ego, the Pinnacle have provided us with the following mantra: "Keep your energy neutral with love as your flow." Being neutral in your energy means being aware of the energy you're reacting to, putting out, or trying to avoid. Being neutral in your energy helps you find your Middle Space, so you can honestly and lovingly look at your emotional responses to what you see and experience in the world as clues to things you need to address within yourself. This is your inner work and the spirituality of the New World. We are beings of polarity; we must honor our shadow as much as we do our light. It is from both sides within us that we grow and evolve. You can love yourself for your shadow as much as your light because both teach you more about how you can shine as your aligned self.

Whatever energy you choose to feed will grow within you and in the energetic field of our planet. The world will continue to change, you will continue to learn, and your energy will continue to move. You will continue to receive messages, and you will choose to follow them or ignore them. You will make decisions that are in alignment and out of alignment. You will feed low vibrational energy, you will feed high vibrational energy. But the more you practice seeing the world through an energetic lens, the more you'll learn the reasons behind your emotional responses to the energy we all feel. You will learn how to look at yourself with love and energetic neutrality. You will see how you are one pixel in the mural of all of humanity. When you align with the New World frequency your pixel will light up and you will shine in all your divine glory, spreading light to those around you.

When we look at the world knowing only our physical nature, we see difference among us. We primarily perceive how we look different, talk different, believe in different things, and live different lives. Difference is a strength of our species, but so often humanity treats difference as a threat. We need to come together in love for one another in all our differences.

The New World frequency is supporting us in our soul work so we can see the energetic connections that unite all physical beings on this planet. The messages of every person who has ever lived on this planet were activated by the energy of the Earth, woven together beneath our feet like a patchwork of memories. We walk on these seams every single day, receiving the energetic reminders through our Line to walk in reverence for our home and in love for one another. When we use this love to come closer in connection with ourselves and others, it is the start of a collective transformation for the New World.

STEP LIGHTLY, LIVE LIGHTLY

One of the great energetic contrasts of this New World is the health of our planet: a changing climate, warming oceans, loss of biodiversity, and an increase in the frequency and intensity of natural disasters that threaten the survival of communities around the world. We are seeing firsthand what it's like to live out of alignment with the planet and with a complete disregard for the sacred energy of Mother Earth.

Looking at this with the long historical perspective of the planet, this will be another one of Earth's cycles, but one that we have directly contributed to. Mother Nature will heal herself. She will move through this cycle and regenerate as she has before. As a species, we need to heal alongside her, for our survival.

The world is a mirror, and the Earth is showing us that we, as a collective, are energetically sick and need to heal. We are deeply disconnected from ourselves. We've been ignoring our messages for too long, numbing ourselves to our emotions, and letting our egos keep us in the same harmful patterns. The New World frequency is supporting our individual healing so we can learn how to come together in a new way and live in alignment with the Earth. When you energetically heal yourself, you're also repairing your energetic relationship with the Earth. This is the necessary first step for all of us if we want to see long-lasting change in our personal and collective physical relationships with the Earth.

I regularly receive messages from people wanting to know what the Pinnacle can tell them about what will happen in the future. Will we be alright? I empathize with every person who sends a message like this. They are looking for something that gives them hope. Many people are living in fear and anxiety about what's to come. They feel like their personal actions won't make a difference on a global scale. For this reason, the Pinnacle's advice often leaves people wanting more. The Pinnacle say that everything begins with you. Each of us needs to be more receptive to our messages, to take personal responsibility for what we can do, and to walk on this Earth in love and alignment.

If you, like many others, struggle to believe your personal actions can make a difference, consider two things. First, the New World frequency came to our planet at this time for a reason. It's supporting the aligned actions of people across the world to create massive global change—and not only with the climate. You can use your Line to receive soul-specific information on how you can begin to energetically heal yourself and your relationship with the planet, including the practical changes you can make in your life to live in alignment with the Earth.

Second, you can have great faith in the impact your actions can make because, just like the New World frequency, you are here on this physical plane at this time for a reason. Use the miraculous gift of Earth Activations to see yourself in the planet, to observe her seasons as a reflection of your own cycles, to feel her energy in your physical body, and to remind yourself that your messages are coming from the Earth. Without her, we wouldn't be able to receive our messages. Connect to this truth and deeply feel it within your heart and essence. Come home to yourself and listen to your messages on the consistent, daily changes you can make in your life to walk in reverence with our shared home, Mother Earth.

This doesn't mean we will each be doing something different and have no way of working together on a common goal. We should come together, but it needs to be from a place of alignment with the energetic root of a changing climate *and* the physical reality of this crisis on Earth.

Whenever there's a massive flood or a surge in the near-constant forest fires, a lot of people in the spiritual community hold mass meditations to shift the frequency of the planet. The hope is that the strong energetic frequency produced by thousands of people meditating will provide physical relief for the Earth and people. When I've asked on behalf of our community if mass meditations and energy work can help support the healing of our planet, the Pinnacle said, "Yes, meditate to remain calm and receive perspective on the situation, but you need to make changes in your daily lifestyle to heal this issue. Step lightly, live lightly."

The last sentence is like a mantra for aligned living in the New World. When you're acting on your messages, you're energetically aligned to your Highest Self and the frequency of this time. This energy will guide you to discover practical ways you can step lightly on this planet. Living lightly frees you from your ego that's trying to keep you the same. It's staying safe that's pulling you out of alignment. When you live lightly, you're nimble, able to shift and change in response to the fluidity of your energy. You can change your patterns, you can try new things, you can have fun. Living lightly is how you heal yourself and heal the planet.

YOU ARE A SEED, SOFTEN TO THIS NEW FREQUENCY

In the New World there is a growing divide between those who are awakened to this new frequency of love and connection and those who only see the physical world. You are being supported in this time to open up to your greatness. It is being revealed to you and you are discovering it. As you continue your soul journey, you must pinpoint what it is you want to know. What do you want to discover? Let your curiosity flow and use your Line as your guide.

As the Pinnacle have said, "Step into the world as if it is brand new, for it is, and you are discovering everything anew. You see that everything is glittering in gold. You know that others do not see what you see but you see the beauty, the newness, the possibility, the opportunity. You see the chance. You see through love, and this is new. It may not be new for you, your soul already knows, but stepping into this time with this intention allows you to grow. It is a mindset you must practice, a mindset you must cultivate, a decision you must nourish, nurture, and be attentive to."

In this new frequency you are like a seed being planted in the Earth. You need to focus on yourself, take care of yourself, and nurture your own growth because when you look to someone else no one is taking care of you.

A seed is firm before it's planted. When you put it in the dirt, it softens from the moisture of the Earth. The seed must maintain this softness for a plant to emerge. If it were left on top of the earth, it would become dry and hard, and the shoots wouldn't be able to break through. Just like the seed you must soften to yourself, your messages, and this new frequency so you can transform.

Our messages come through and we receive them and want to act on them. We have a plan on how we'll act on them, but then for some reason we harden to that. We create reasons we can't do it. We resist ourselves, even if that resistance comes in the form of a distraction. You pick up your phone to check something, and then suddenly you're looking at the weather, then the news, then social media, and then forty-five minutes have gone by and that window of time when you wanted to act on your message has passed. Then you think, "I just don't have the time."

Your messages are coming to you at the perfect time, but the moment you doubt yourself, you begin to harden to your message and to the energy you felt when the message came through. The energy that was supporting your action has shifted. You can always find your way back to that frequency, but when you trust that in every moment you have everything you need to act on your messages, you will soften.

You go through cycles within yourself when you're acting on your messages and when you're not. When you're resistant and harden to them, you don't die like a seed in a drought. You can always sprout and continue growing, but you need that soft connection with yourself, and that comes from witnessing your transformations and allowing yourself to see the miracles of this life. To transform, you need to act on your messages. To act on your messages, you need to love yourself and trust the divine guidance coming through.

When you soften to your messages, you are opening your heart to this New World frequency and to the beauty all around you. It's how you experience the feeling of connection to yourself, how you see yourself as part of Mother Earth and one with the collective energy she holds.

When you're soft, you can absorb new experiences, new ideas, and new energy that your messages bring. They don't bounce off you right away. The absorption is slow, and you have time to understand, to process, to learn, and to grow. You can absorb pain when you're in the discomfort of change. Soften to your messages, your Line, and the frequency of this New World, and you will transform.

Right now, you may feel like you're a seed in the dark, so I want you to remember that you grow in the dark. Be present and look to yourself. What are you receiving? How are you to respond?

Listen to yourself. This is a new way of living.

APPENDIX

PRAYER OF THE NEW WORLD

In April 2020, I channeled the Prayer of the New World in my Akashic Records. This prayer brings us to a new realm within the Akashic Records; a realm that includes the Earth frequency and the New World frequency. Our Akashic Records are stored in the Pleaides and, up until channeling this prayer, I was always traveling up to receive information and guidance from the Records. This prayer combines both energies, the sky above and the Earth below, in addition to the New World frequency, to provide a much more grounded and powerful experience within the Records. It is a prayer of compassion that supports deep introspection and self-healing. As we heal ourselves through this frequency, we also heal the Earth. I recommend doing a Line Activation before you use this prayer to help you feel centered and grounded. Recite the Opening Prayer to enter the Records and the Closing Prayer to exit the Records. Each prayer should be spoken out loud, either with your eyes open or closed.

OPENING PRAYER

We gather together in light. We gather together in love. We gather together in knowing the messages from above. Through the Akashic Records, we understand our greatness. Through the Akashic Records we understand our wisdom. Through the Akashic Records, we understand what's there. This prayer will help deliver us there.

I wish to know (myself/client's name/animal's name/location) in the light of the Akashic Records. Help me to see (myself/client's name/animal's name/ location) through the light of the Akashic Records. Bring me to feel (myself/ client's name/animal's name/location) through the light of the Akashic Records.

I wish to know (myself/client's name/animal's name/location) in the light of the Akashic Records. Help me to see (myself/client's name/

animal's name/location) through the light of the Akashic Records. Bring me to feel (myself/client's name/animal's name/location) through the light of the Akashic Records.

And now the Akashic Records are open.

CLOSING PRAYER

I give gratitude to (myself/client's name/animal's name/location) for entering the Records. I give gratitude to the Pinnacle for lighting the way. I give gratitude to this space for the comfort and love. I give gratitude to (my/client name's/animal name's/location's) Highest Self for leading (me or us) here. The Records are now closed, amen. The Records are now closed, amen. The Records are now closed, amen.

For complete instruction on how to read the Akashic Records with the Prayer of the New World for yourself and others and how to build an online business as an Akashic Records reader, refer to our course How to Read the Akashic Records with the Pinnacle on alnwithin.com.

ACKNOWLEDGMENTS

Thank you to the Pinnacle for channeling this wisdom through me. I am honored to be a conduit to share it with the world.

Ben, when we began writing this book we were married. Now we are not. Through this process of this creation, we learned that our soul contract as husband and wife had ended and so our relationship changed. Thank you for being my cocreator on this project (and many others) and for your friendship. Thank you for your tough love and tenderness. Thank you for your endurance and strength. At times writing this book felt like climbing the tallest mountain and without you, it wouldn't be what it is. Thank you for bringing your wisdom, your skill, your talent, your heart and your stamina to this project. One of your goals in this life is to "help people get where they're going" and the amount of space and energy you can hold for me is astounding. I will always love you.

My sweet daughter, Baboo, love of my life. The moment our souls conneced my life was forever changed. Words cannot express how grateful I am for you. Thank you for sharing a new level of love with me and for all of the wisdom you've gifted me thus far. You are my greatest teacher, and it's an honor to guide you in this life.

Feesh and Bose, my kitties and light guides. Thank you for sitting with me, for sharing messages with me, for healing me, and for unconditionally loving me. As humans, our relationship with animals is so sacred, and I love you both so deeply.

Talluah, my baby kitten and little Pleiadian twinkling star. You moved into our home the week before we completed this book, but I am already so in love with you and honored to experience your life's work alongside you.

Bev Morden and Val Wood, thank you for taking care of Baboo while Ben and I worked away on this project. Thank you for keeping up with her, for sharing your love with her, and for always making her feel special. Grant Morden and Ron Wood, thank you for sharing your wives with us so often. I love you all.

Thank you to the Sounds True team and to my editor, Jaime Schwalb. During our first call together, I recalled a moment back in 2013 when I had just started food blogging and was holding a cookbook by another blogger that had just been released. "Wow, it would be so amazing to write a book," I thought. Within the brief moment of recalling that memory, I heard through my Line, "You asked for this, here you go; enjoy writing your book." Thank you for taking action on your message to approach me to write the book and for all of your support, encouragement, and understanding along the way.

Guru Jagat, thank you for your spirit that continues to wrap around the world in expansive love and wisdom, even after your physical body left this plane. It was through a message to do kundalini yoga (obsessively) for a few months that led me to the moment of receiving this message midpractice one day: "Stop what you're doing—this is the Line Activation; teach this to the world." Without the RA MA Institute for Applied Yogic Science and Technology as a space for learning, I wouldn't have received the Line Activation—a beautiful example of how our messages are stepping stones.

Laura Ohta, Leslie Galbraith, and Purnima Chaudhari, my soul sisters; words cannot express how grateful I am to have found you in this life. Thank you for the wisdom you've bestowed upon me and the love and support you've always shown me. You inspire me, comfort me, and truly feel like family to me. I'm so grateful for the beautiful alignments our souls create in the cosmos together.

Kelsey Ammon, my shining star, thank you for everything you bring to my life, to A Line Within, and for taking the time to read this book before anyone else could! Thank you for your love, your honest feedback, and for the beautiful light that you bring into my life and this world. You are my teacher, my friend, and I'm so grateful to have you in my life.

Jessica Kraft, thank you for your comprehensive edit of this book, for the honest, clear, and supportive feedback that inspired a complete rewrite, and for challenging me to create an even better book. I appreciate your contribution to this project so much. Jill Rogers, thank you for your insightful and supportive copyedits on this project. Laurel Szmyd and the rest of the Sounds True production team, thank you for seeing out the publication of this book.

Tanya Montpetit, I came to you with a big job, and you pulled it off with ease. Thank you for taking a vision I had and bringing it to life by designing the most beautiful book cover. Your talent and ability to create ethereal, vibrant, mystical, and grounded art is so inspiring to me, and I am grateful to work alongside you on this project and the many creations that A Line Within produces. Thank you, thank you, thank you!

Vanessa Mayberry, thank you for bringing your talent, kind heart, and fun to the many days that we spent outside attempting to take the "perfect" author photo. After hundreds of photos and a few different locations, you took the most beautiful photo that doesn't only show the "physical" me but also captures my soul essence. Thank you so much!

Kami Speer, the soul connection we share is so special to me. Thank you for channeling the most beautiful Aurora dress for me within the energy of the Great Conjunction, as Saturn and Jupiter were coming together in Aquarius. This garment holds such a powerful frequency and, as you know, brought soul experiences into my awareness the moment I put it on my body. It's for this reason that wearing it in my author photo is the reason my soul shines through. Deep gratitude.

Jaxson Pohlman, thank you for entering my life in divine timing, for teaching me a new understanding of compassion that deeply influenced how I wrote this book, for bringing me soul-family love (and being the first to teach me about it), and for mirroring back to me the gifts that are within me. I am grateful for you.

Juuso Hämäläinen, we only just met as I was finishing this book, but I can already tell how significant our connection is, however long it lasts in this life. I am so grateful for you, for what we have shared, and for what I have learned from and through you already. You are so special to me.

Mother Earth, thank you for holding me, healing me, and endlessly inspiring me. I will forever step lightly in reverence for your glory. I am so grateful to not only see you but to also feel you.

Infinite sky above, thank you for taking my breath away every single night from the soul-deep, activating magic I receive standing beneath you. I see home within you, and I'm forever grateful to experience and receive you from this Earth plane perspective.

Thank you to our loyal, loving, and supportive A Line Within community. Thank you for sharing your energy with us and for growing alongside us.

And, of course, thank you, dark chocolate, for always being there for me when I needed you.

NOTES

1. Anthony F. Aveni, *Skywatchers* (Austin: University of Texas Press, 2001), 29–33.

2. Hesiod, *Works and Days*, line 615, Perseus Digital Library, Tufts University, accessed March 18, 2021, perseus.tufts.edu/hopper /text?doc=Perseus%3Atext%3A1999.01.0132%3Acard%3D609.

3. Aveni, *Skywatchers,* 30.

4. Brian Haughton, "The Nebra Sky Disk—Ancient Map of the Stars," *World History Encyclopedia*, May 10, 2011, ancient.eu /article/235/the-nebra-sky-disk---ancient-map-of-the-stars/

ABOUT THE
AUTHOR

Ashley Wood is the cofounder, alongside Ben Wood, of A Line Within and host of *The Line* podcast. She lives under the Northern Lights in Manitoba, Canada, with her daughter, three cats, and many woodland forest creatures.

ABOUT
SOUNDS TRUE

S ounds True is a multimedia publisher whose mission is to inspire and support personal transformation and spiritual awakening. Founded in 1985 and located in Boulder, Colorado, we work with many of the leading spiritual teachers, thinkers, healers, and visionary artists of our time. We strive with every title to preserve the essential "living wisdom" of the author or artist. It is our goal to create products that not only provide information to a reader or listener but also embody the quality of a wisdom transmission.

For those seeking genuine transformation, Sounds True is your trusted partner. At SoundsTrue.com you will find a wealth of free resources to support your journey, including exclusive weekly audio interviews, free downloads, interactive learning tools, and other special savings on all our titles.

To learn more, please visit SoundsTrue.com/freegifts or call us toll-free at 800.333.9185.

sounds true
WAKING UP THE WORLD